AI for Students

Learn Smarter, Not Easier — AI Tools for Research, Writing, and Academic Success

Ken Tannenbaum

2026

Finnoybu Press

AI for Students

2026 Edition

Learn Smarter, Not Easier — AI Tools for Research, Writing, and Academic Success

---

Published by Finnoybu Press

For permissions and inquiries: press@finnoybu.org

First Edition: 2026

About the Author

Ken Tannenbaum is a technologist, entrepreneur, and AI governance researcher. He is the founder of Finnoybu Press and the founder/steward of the AEGIS Initiative, an open framework for AI safety and accountability. Learn more at aegis-initiative.com.

When he's not building governance standards for artificial intelligence, he's helping everyday people understand and use it.

Dedication

For every student who's been told to "just figure it out."

School teaches you subjects, but nobody teaches you how to learn — how to read a dense paper, how to unstick yourself at midnight when a concept won't click, how to organize research that's piling up faster than you can process it.

This book is for that gap. The tools in these pages won't replace the work — nothing will, and nothing should. But they can make the work less lonely, less confusing, and a lot more productive.

You've got this.

The AI for Everyone Series

This book is part of the **AI for Everyone** series by Finnoybu Press, designed to help real people use AI tools effectively. Visit **press.finnoybu.org** for the latest titles and updates.

Collection One: Product Deep Dives

- *ChatGPT: The Definitive Guide (2026 Edition)*
- *ChatGPT: The Power User Guide (2026 Edition)*
- *Claude: The Definitive Guide (2026 Edition)*
- *Claude Code: The Power User Guide (2026 Edition)*
- *Gemini: The Complete Guide (2026 Edition)*
- *Gemini: The Advanced Guide (2026 Edition)*
- *Copilot: The Workplace AI Guide (2026 Edition)*
- *Copilot: The Advanced Workplace Guide (2026 Edition)*
- *Perplexity: The Research Playbook (2026 Edition)*
- *Perplexity: The Advanced Research Playbook (2026 Edition)*

Collection Two: Product Guides

- *NotebookLM: From Sources to Audio Overviews (2026 Edition)*
- *DeepSeek: Code, Math, and Reasoning (2026 Edition)*
- *Cursor: The AI Code Editor (2026 Edition)*
- *OpenClaw: Agentic AI for Everyday Work (2026 Edition)*

Collection Three: Cross-Platform Skills

- *AI Systems Playbook (2026 Edition)*
- *AI Prompt Engineering (2026 Edition)*
- *AI for Developers (2026 Edition)*
- *AI for Business (2026 Edition)*
- *AI for Students (2026 Edition)*
- *AI Governance for Practitioners (2026 Edition)*
- *Securing Agentic AI (2026 Edition)*

Table of Contents

Introduction

Why This Book Exists

You already know AI is a big deal. You've probably used it — maybe for homework, maybe to write something, maybe just to see what the fuss is about. Your professors and teachers have opinions about it, ranging from enthusiastic adoption to outright bans. Your classmates are using it, talking about it, and in some cases getting in trouble for it.

What you probably don't have is a clear, honest guide to using AI well as a student.

That's what this book is.

Not a sales pitch for any particular AI tool. Not a breathless manifesto about how AI will change everything. And not a lecture about how you're all going to become cheaters. This is a practical guide for students — high school through graduate school — who want to use AI to learn more effectively, research more efficiently, and produce better academic work without crossing ethical lines.

Who This Book Is For

This book is written for three audiences:

High school students who are encountering AI tools for the first time and need to understand what's available, what's allowed, and how to use these tools without getting into trouble. You're at the stage where learning habits are forming, and the habits you build around AI now will follow you into college and beyond.

Undergraduate students who face the most complex AI landscape. Your professors have wildly different policies. Some classes encourage AI use; others forbid it entirely. You need to produce original work, develop expertise in your field, and graduate with skills that matter — all while navigating tools that make it tempting to take shortcuts.

Graduate students and researchers who operate under the highest standards of academic integrity but also have the most to gain from AI-assisted research. Literature reviews, data analysis, methodology design, thesis writing — AI can accelerate all of it, but only if you use it in ways your institution and your field consider legitimate.

No matter which group you belong to, the core challenge is the same: how do you use these powerful tools responsibly?

What This Book Covers

We start with the landscape — what AI tools are available to you in 2026 and what each one is good at. Then we tackle the hardest topic head-on: academic integrity. Chapter 3 is the most important chapter in this book, and I won't sugarcoat it. Using AI to bypass learning isn't just against the rules; it's bad for you. That chapter gives you a clear framework for knowing where the line is.

From there, we get practical. Using AI to understand concepts better. Doing research with AI that makes your literature reviews stronger, not lazier. Writing papers where AI helps you become a better writer rather than replacing your voice. Studying for exams. Working through math and science problems. Analyzing literature and history. Coding. Group projects. Presentations. Graduate-level research.

We also cover the stuff nobody else talks about. What to do when a professor bans AI and you disagree with the policy. How to protect your privacy when using AI tools. How to handle it when AI gives you wrong information — because it will. How to manage subscriptions on a student budget. How AI skills translate into career value after graduation.

The appendices are designed as reference material you'll actually use: prompt templates organized by subject, citation formats for AI-assisted work, a glossary, and a resource list.

The Academic Integrity Commitment

Let me be direct about something. This book will teach you things that, if misused, could help you cheat. I know that. I wrote the book anyway because the alternative — students fumbling through AI use with no guidance — is worse.

Here is my commitment to you: everything in this book is written with academic integrity as a non-negotiable constraint. When I show you how to use AI for a research paper, I show you how to do it in a way your professor could watch over your shoulder without objection. When I give you prompt templates, they're designed to help you learn, not to generate submissions. When a technique could cross an ethical line, I tell you exactly where that line is.

In return, I need something from you: honesty. Not with me — I'll never know how you use what's in these pages. Honesty with yourself. The student who uses AI to understand a concept they were struggling with has gained something real. The student who pastes an assignment into ChatGPT and submits the output has gained nothing except risk.

You're smart enough to know the difference. This book assumes that about you.

How to Read This Book

You don't have to read this cover to cover, though it's designed to work that way. If you're in a hurry:

- **If you just need to know what's allowed**, read Chapters 3, 18, and 19.
- **If you want to use AI for a paper due next week**, read Chapters 5 and 6.
- **If you're studying for exams**, jump to Chapter 7.
- **If you're a grad student**, start with Chapter 13 and work backward.
- **If you need prompt templates right now**, go to Appendix A.

But if you have the time, start at Chapter 1. Understanding the bigger picture of AI in education will make every other chapter more useful.

A Note About Accuracy

The AI landscape changes constantly. New models launch monthly, features get added, prices shift, and best practices evolve. This book is accurate as of May 2026, but specific details — vendor pricing, feature availability, exact tool capabilities — may have shifted by the time you read this.

The principles, techniques, and strategies in this book have a longer shelf life than the specific tool details. How to use AI to deepen learning, conduct research with integrity, and develop habits that make you a better student — those skills transfer across versions and even across different AI tools.

When something looks different from what's described here, check the vendor's documentation for the latest information.

Let's Get Started

You're entering college and careers in a world where AI is embedded in almost every professional workflow. The students who thrive won't be the ones who avoided AI or relied on it as a crutch. They'll be the ones who learned to use it as a tool — thoughtfully, ethically, and effectively.

That's what we're here to learn. Let's go.

Part I: AI and Academic Life

"Education is not the filling of a pail, but the lighting of a fire."

— W. B. Yeats (attributed)

Chapter 1: AI in Education: Where We Are

The Semester Everything Changed

If you started college before November 2022, you remember the before. Research meant library databases and Google Scholar. Writing meant staring at a blank document. Studying meant rereading notes and hoping something stuck. Help meant office hours, tutoring centers, or texting a friend who might know the answer.

Then ChatGPT launched, and within weeks, every student on every campus had access to a tool that could generate essays, solve math problems, write code, explain complex concepts, and produce work that was, frankly, hard to distinguish from student-written material.

The response from educational institutions was — predictably — messy. Some schools banned AI entirely. Others embraced it immediately. Most fell somewhere in the confused middle, scrambling to update academic integrity policies for a technology most administrators didn't fully understand.

That was three years ago. In 2026, we're past the panic phase but not yet in the settled phase. AI in education is real, permanent, and still being figured out. This chapter is about where we stand.

The Current State of Play

As of early 2026, here's what the landscape looks like:

Most universities now have official AI policies. The era of professors making up rules on the fly is mostly over. Major institutions — the University of California system, the Ivy League, Big Ten schools, the Russell Group in the UK — have published institution-wide frameworks for AI use. These policies generally establish a spectrum: some assignments allow AI, some don't, and professors have the authority to set rules for their specific courses.

High schools are catching up. K–12 adoption has been slower and more cautious, partly because of concerns about developmental impact on younger students and partly because high school teachers have less autonomy in setting technology policy. Most school districts now have some form of AI guidance, but it varies widely by state, district, and even individual school.

AI detection tools exist but aren't reliable. This matters: tools like Turnitin's AI detection, GPTZero, and others can flag text that might be AI-generated, but they produce both false positives (flagging human-written work as AI) and false negatives (missing AI-generated text). No institution that takes fairness seriously relies solely on detection software. If your school does, that's a problem — and we'll cover how to handle it in Chapter 18.

The tools have improved dramatically. In 2023, AI could write a decent essay but struggled with nuance, citation accuracy, and sustained argumentation. In 2026, the leading AI models produce work that is sophisticated, well-structured, and dangerously convincing — even when it's wrong. This makes the integrity question harder, not easier.

Students are using AI whether institutions like it or not. Every survey of student AI use tells the same story: the vast majority of students have used AI for academic work. Use ranges from fully legitimate (asking an AI to explain a concept) to clearly illegitimate (submitting AI-generated work as your own). Most use falls somewhere in the middle, in a gray area this book exists to illuminate.

Why Schools Are Struggling with This

To understand why AI policies are all over the map, it helps to understand what schools are trying to protect.

Learning itself. The point of education isn't to produce essays — it's to develop your ability to think, analyze, argue, and create. When AI writes your paper, you skip the cognitive process the paper was designed to trigger. A chemistry professor who assigns lab reports isn't trying to assess your ability to format a document; they want you to process what happened in the lab. An English professor who assigns an essay on *Beloved* wants you to wrestle with the text, not outsource the wrestling.

Assessment validity. Grades are supposed to reflect what you know and can do. If AI does the work, your grade reflects what AI can do, which isn't useful information for anyone — not your professors, not graduate admissions committees, not future employers, and not you.

Equity. Not all students have equal access to AI tools. Paid subscriptions to ChatGPT Plus, Claude Pro, or Gemini Advanced cost $20 per month — a meaningful expense for many students. If AI use gives an academic advantage, students who can afford subscriptions have an edge over those who can't. Schools worry about creating a two-tier system.

Institutional credibility. A degree from your school is supposed to mean something. If it becomes known that students routinely use AI to produce their work, the value of that degree erodes — which hurts every student and alumnus, not just the ones who used AI.

These aren't arbitrary concerns. They're real problems. The tension you feel — between AI being useful and these real risks — isn't going to resolve neatly. But it can be navigated thoughtfully, which is what this book is about.

What Different Institutions Are Doing

The policy landscape in 2026 broadly falls into four categories:

The Restrictive Approach

Some institutions and departments have decided the risks outweigh the benefits, at least for certain courses. You'll encounter this most in introductory courses, standardized testing, and disciplines where the process of producing work is the entire pedagogical point — creative writing workshops, proof-based math courses, philosophy seminars.

These policies typically prohibit any AI use on submitted work and may include proctored exams, in-class writing, and oral defenses to verify students can demonstrate competence independently.

If you think this approach is wrong, you might be right — but it's not unreasonable, and Chapter 18 will help you work within it productively.

The Permissive Approach

Other institutions, particularly in professional and technical programs, have fully embraced AI as a tool students should learn to use. Computer science departments, business schools, data science programs, and some engineering programs increasingly treat AI fluency as a learning objective in itself.

These policies typically allow or encourage AI use with disclosure requirements — you must document what tools you used and how. Some require you to submit your AI interaction logs alongside your work.

Chapter 19 covers how to thrive in this environment.

The Graduated Approach

The most common institutional framework in 2026 is graduated: AI use is regulated per-course or per-assignment, with professors setting specific policies. An introductory writing course might ban AI entirely, while an upper-level research seminar in the same department might require it.

This is probably the approach you're dealing with. It means you need to read every syllabus carefully, ask questions when policies are unclear, and never assume what's allowed in one class applies to another.

The Unspoken Approach

Some schools — particularly smaller institutions and under-resourced districts — still don't have clear policies. This is the hardest situation to navigate because the rules are ambiguous. Chapter 3 gives you an ethical framework that works even when institutional guidance is missing.

The Technology Side

AI in education isn't just about chatbots. The technology ecosystem now includes:

General-purpose AI assistants like ChatGPT, Claude, and Gemini, which can help with nearly any academic task from writing to coding to research.

Search-focused AI tools like Perplexity, which combine AI reasoning with real-time web search and source citation — making them particularly useful for research.

Specialized academic tools like Consensus (AI-powered academic search), Elicit (research assistant), Semantic Scholar (AI-enhanced paper discovery), and

Scite (citation analysis). These are designed for scholarly work and are generally considered more acceptable in academic settings.

Note-taking and synthesis tools like Google's NotebookLM, which can analyze documents you upload and help you synthesize information from your own sources.

Coding assistants like GitHub Copilot, which autocomplete and generate code — raising their own integrity questions in computer science courses.

Writing assistants like Grammarly, which have added AI features that go well beyond spell-checking into rewriting and content generation.

AI-enhanced learning platforms like Khan Academy's Khanmigo, which use AI to provide personalized tutoring within a pedagogically designed framework.

Chapter 2 breaks all of these down in detail. The point here is that "AI in education" is not one thing — it's a sprawling ecosystem of tools with different capabilities, different risks, and different levels of institutional acceptance.

The Numbers

Let's look at what the research tells us about AI use in education as of early 2026:

Student usage is near-universal. Multiple large-scale surveys — including studies from the Stanford Digital Education group, EDUCAUSE, and JISC — report that over 85% of university students have used generative AI tools for some form of academic work. Usage rates are highest among STEM students and graduate students, but no demographic is below 60%.

Most use is supplementary, not substitutive. The same surveys show most students use AI as a study aid (explaining concepts, generating practice questions) rather than to produce submitted work. The feared epidemic of wholesale AI-generated submissions has not materialized at the scale initially predicted — though it happens, and it's a real problem.

Faculty adoption is growing. About 60% of university faculty now use AI in some aspect of their work — research, course design, or grading support. Faculty who use AI themselves tend to have more nuanced policies for students.

Academic integrity cases involving AI have stabilized. After a spike in 2023–2024, the number of AI-related academic integrity cases has plateaued at most institutions. This likely reflects a mix of clearer policies, better student understanding, and institutions realizing detection tools aren't reliable enough to build cases on.

Employer expectations are shifting. This matters for you: surveys of employers consistently show AI literacy is now among the top five skills they look for in new graduates, across virtually every industry. The gap between how schools treat AI and how employers treat AI is real and growing.

The Uncomfortable Truth

Here's something most books on this topic won't say directly: the current system is incoherent.

Schools simultaneously tell you AI is transforming every industry, that you need to be prepared for an AI-driven workplace, and that you shouldn't use AI for your academic work. They tell you to develop AI literacy while punishing you for demonstrating it in the wrong context. They acknowledge AI tools are becoming as fundamental as calculators and word processors while treating their use as potential misconduct.

This isn't a criticism of any particular institution. It's an honest assessment of a system in transition. Education is figuring out AI in real time, and the contradictions are real.

Your job as a student isn't to resolve these contradictions — it's to navigate them. That means understanding both the legitimate concerns behind restrictive policies and the value of AI as a learning tool. It means being strategic about when and how you use AI. It means developing the skills AI can't replace while leveraging AI for the tasks where it helps.

That's what the rest of this book teaches you to do.

What's at Stake for You

This isn't abstract. The choices you make about AI in the next few years will shape real outcomes:

Your actual learning. If you use AI as a shortcut, you'll graduate with a degree but without the skills it's supposed to represent. That gap shows up — in job interviews, in professional performance, in your own confidence.

Your academic record. An academic integrity violation can follow you for years. It can affect graduate school admissions, professional licensing, and employment. The consequences are real and often disproportionate.

Your professional readiness. Conversely, if you develop real skill in using AI as a professional tool — not a crutch, but a multiplier — you'll enter the workforce with a significant advantage. The students who figure out how to learn with AI, not instead of AI, are going to do very well.

Your relationship with technology. The habits you build now around AI will persist. Students who learn to use AI thoughtfully become professionals who use AI thoughtfully. Students who learn to depend on AI uncritically become professionals who depend on AI uncritically — and those professionals make expensive mistakes.

Moving Forward

The rest of this book is organized around a simple idea: AI is a tool, and like every tool, its value depends on how you use it. A calculator doesn't make you a mathematician. Spell-check doesn't make you a writer. A power saw doesn't make you a carpenter. But if you're learning to be a mathematician, a writer, or a carpenter, these tools can make your learning faster, your practice more effective, and your output better.

AI is a more powerful tool than any of those examples, which means both the potential benefits and the potential harms are larger. The stakes are higher. And the skill of using it well is correspondingly more valuable.

Let's start building that skill.

Chapter 2: The AI Tools Available to You

The Toolbox

Walk into a hardware store and you'll find a hundred different tools, each designed for a specific job. You could probably hammer a screw into wood if you tried hard enough, but a screwdriver works better. AI tools are the same way. There are a lot of them, they overlap, and picking the right one for the job makes a real difference.

This chapter is your map of what's available in 2026, what each tool is best at, what it costs, and which ones are worth your attention as a student. I'll be direct about strengths and weaknesses because you don't have unlimited time or money, and you need honest recommendations.

The Big Four: General-Purpose AI Assistants

These are the tools that can do almost anything — answer questions, write text, analyze documents, solve problems, generate code. They're the Swiss Army knives of AI.

ChatGPT (by OpenAI)

What it is: The tool that started the wave. ChatGPT is a conversational AI that handles text generation, analysis, coding, math, and more. As of 2026, the latest models include GPT-5.4 and dedicated reasoning variants.

Free tier: ChatGPT Free gives you access to GPT-5.4 with usage limits. You can have conversations, ask questions, upload files, and use basic features. When you hit the limit, it drops you to a less capable model. For many student tasks, the free tier is enough.

Paid tier: ChatGPT Plus costs $20/month and gives you higher usage limits, access to the GPT-5.4 reasoning variants for complex problems, more file uploads, and priority access during peak times.

Best for: General-purpose academic help, writing assistance, coding, brainstorming. ChatGPT has the largest ecosystem of integrations and the most third-party resources written about it.

Weaknesses: Can be verbose. Tends to agree with you even when you're wrong (sycophancy). Citation accuracy is inconsistent — never trust a source it gives you without verifying it yourself.

Student verdict: A solid default choice. The free tier handles most tasks. Worth exploring before paying for anything else.

Claude (by Anthropic)

What it is: Anthropic's AI assistant, known for longer, more thoughtful responses and strong performance on complex reasoning tasks. Claude's latest models (the Opus and Sonnet families as of early 2026) are particularly strong at nuanced analysis and careful instruction-following.

Free tier: Claude.ai offers free access with usage limits. You can have conversations, upload documents, and use basic features. Limits reset periodically.

Paid tier: Claude Pro costs $20/month and provides much higher usage limits, access to the most capable models, and additional features like Projects (organized workspaces for different classes or research areas).

Best for: Long-form analysis, careful reasoning, document review, research synthesis, and tasks where you want thoughtful rather than surface-level responses. Claude is more willing to say "I'm not sure" or flag uncertainty, which is valuable in academic contexts.

Weaknesses: Smaller ecosystem than ChatGPT — fewer tutorials and third-party integrations. Can be overly cautious or hedge too much.

Student verdict: Excellent for research and analytical writing. The Projects feature is useful for organizing academic work. Strong recommendation for graduate students.

Gemini (by Google)

What it is: Google's AI platform, deeply integrated with the Google ecosystem — Gmail, Docs, Drive, Search, YouTube, and Maps. The latest models (Gemini 3.1 Pro as of mid-2026) are multimodal, meaning they handle text, images, audio, and video.

Free tier: Gemini is free with a Google account, which you almost certainly already have. The free tier includes strong capabilities and tight integration with Google Workspace.

Paid tier: Google One AI Premium costs $20/month and includes Gemini Advanced (more capable models), Gemini in Google Workspace apps (Docs, Sheets, Slides, Gmail), and 2TB of Google storage.

Best for: Students who live in the Google ecosystem. If you use Google Docs for papers, Google Slides for presentations, and Gmail for communication, Gemini's integrations are powerful. Also strong for multimodal tasks — analyzing images, working with videos, processing audio recordings of lectures.

Weaknesses: Responses can feel less polished than ChatGPT or Claude for pure writing tasks. The integration with Google services is both a strength and a privacy concern (more on that in Chapter 16).

Student verdict: If you're already a Google Workspace user, the free tier is a no-brainer. The paid tier is the best value because it bundles AI with storage and workspace integration.

Microsoft Copilot

What it is: Microsoft's AI offering, integrated with the Microsoft 365 ecosystem — Word, Excel, PowerPoint, Outlook, OneNote, and Teams. Uses OpenAI's models under the hood but with Microsoft's integration layer.

Free tier: Copilot is available for free at copilot.microsoft.com with basic capabilities. It includes web search integration by default.

Paid tier: Copilot Pro costs $20/month and adds AI features directly into Microsoft 365 apps. Microsoft 365 Copilot (the enterprise version) is more expensive and primarily aimed at businesses.

Best for: Students who use Microsoft Office for everything. Having AI directly in Word while you're writing a paper, or in PowerPoint while you're building a presentation, reduces friction. Also useful for Excel-based data analysis.

Weaknesses: The standalone chatbot experience is less refined than ChatGPT or Claude. The real value is in the Office integration, and if you don't use Office, there's less reason to choose Copilot.

Student verdict: Good if your school provides Microsoft 365 (many do). The in-app integration is useful for productivity. Less compelling as a standalone AI assistant.

Research-Focused Tools

These tools are designed for finding and analyzing information, and they're where many students should actually spend their time.

Perplexity

What it is: An AI-powered search engine that answers questions with cited sources. Unlike ChatGPT or Claude, Perplexity searches the web in real time and provides numbered references for its claims.

Free tier: Generous free tier with a limited number of "Pro" searches per day (which use more capable models and deeper analysis). Standard searches are unlimited.

Paid tier: Perplexity Pro costs $20/month and provides unlimited Pro searches, file uploads, and access to multiple AI models.

Best for: Research. When you need factual answers with sources you can verify, Perplexity is the best starting point. It won't replace a proper literature review, but it's excellent for initial exploration of a topic, finding key papers, and getting oriented in an unfamiliar field.

Weaknesses: Weaker for creative or analytical writing tasks. The sources it cites are real (unlike ChatGPT's sometimes-fabricated citations), but that doesn't mean they're the best sources — you still need to evaluate quality.

Student verdict: Highly recommended for every student. The free tier is useful; Pro is worth considering if you do a lot of research. This should be one of your primary tools.

Google NotebookLM

What it is: A research tool that lets you upload documents — PDFs, articles, notes, textbook chapters — and then ask questions about them. NotebookLM works with your sources, not the open internet, which makes it different from a chatbot in a fundamental way.

Free tier: Free with a Google account. Generous limits on sources and queries.

Paid tier: NotebookLM Plus offers higher limits and additional features.

Best for: Synthesizing reading material. Upload your course readings, lecture notes, and research papers, then ask questions about them. It can generate study guides, find connections between sources, create audio overviews (podcast-style summaries), and help you understand dense material. Because it only works with sources you provide, the hallucination risk is much lower.

Weaknesses: Limited to what you upload — it won't search for new information. The audio overview feature is useful but not always accurate in its emphasis.

Student verdict: Underrated. If you're not using NotebookLM for your readings, you're missing out. Especially valuable for courses with heavy reading loads.

Consensus

What it is: An AI search engine specifically for academic papers. It searches a database of over 200 million scholarly articles and synthesizes findings using AI.

Free tier: Limited free searches per month.

Paid tier: Consensus Pro is available for a modest monthly fee — check their current pricing page for the latest rates and any student discounts.

Best for: Literature reviews and finding academic evidence for claims. When you need peer-reviewed sources on a topic, Consensus searches actual academic databases rather than the open web.

Student verdict: Valuable for research papers and thesis work. The free tier is limiting; consider the paid tier if you write research papers regularly.

Semantic Scholar

What it is: An AI-powered academic search engine from the Allen Institute for AI. It provides AI-generated summaries of papers, citation analysis, and research trend tracking.

Free tier: Free. Fully free.

Paid tier: None needed for basic use.

Best for: Finding papers, understanding citation networks, and tracking research trends. The TLDR feature (AI-generated one-sentence summaries of papers) is useful for quickly scanning search results.

Student verdict: Should be in every student's research toolkit. Free, useful, and built for academic work.

Coding Tools

If you write code for any class — computer science, data science, engineering, statistics, or even digital humanities — these tools are relevant.

GitHub Copilot

What it is: An AI coding assistant that integrates into code editors (VS Code, JetBrains, etc.) and suggests code as you type. It can also answer questions about code, debug errors, and explain existing code.

Free tier: GitHub Copilot Free provides limited completions and chat per month. Students can get GitHub Copilot Pro free through the GitHub Student Developer Pack.

Paid tier: Copilot Pro costs $10/month — but again, free for verified students.

Best for: Writing code faster, debugging, understanding unfamiliar codebases, and learning programming concepts through example.

Weaknesses: Can generate code that works but that you don't understand — which defeats the purpose in a learning context. Many CS professors have specific policies about Copilot use.

Student verdict: Get the free student access. Use it to learn, not to bypass learning. We'll cover this more in Chapter 10.

Replit

What it is: An online coding platform with built-in AI assistance. You can write, run, and deploy code in your browser with AI help.

Free tier: Free tier with AI features included.

Best for: Quick coding tasks, learning new languages, and situations where you don't want to set up a local development environment.

Writing and Productivity Tools

Grammarly

What it is: A writing assistant that's been around much longer than generative AI but has incorporated AI features that now go well beyond grammar checking. It can rewrite sentences, adjust tone, and generate text.

Free tier: Basic grammar and spelling checking is free.

Paid tier: Grammarly Premium costs $12/month and includes AI-powered rewriting, tone adjustment, and full-sentence suggestions.

Note: Grammarly exists in a gray area. Using it for grammar checking is universally accepted. Using its AI rewriting features may or may not be allowed under your school's AI policy. Know the difference and act accordingly.

Notion AI

What it is: AI features built into Notion, a popular note-taking and organization platform. Can summarize notes, generate outlines, brainstorm ideas, and assist with writing within your existing Notion workspace.

Paid tier: Requires a Notion subscription plus an AI add-on.

Best for: Students who already use Notion for note-taking and project management.

How to Think About Costs

Let's be real: $20/month is a lot when you're a student. That's $240/year — enough for textbooks, groceries, or a significant chunk of a streaming budget. Here's how to think about it:

Start with free tiers. Every major tool has a free tier that's good enough for most student tasks. Use them. Hit the limits. See which tools you use enough to warrant paying for.

Check for student discounts. GitHub Copilot is free for students. Some tools offer education pricing. Your school may have institutional licenses. Check with your IT department.

Don't subscribe to everything. You don't need ChatGPT Plus and Claude Pro and Gemini Advanced and Perplexity Pro. Pick one general-purpose tool and one research tool, and use the free tiers for everything else.

Explore family plans (where available). Some AI services offer family or group plans at a lower per-person cost. Check each platform's current offerings and terms of service — sharing individual account credentials is generally prohibited, but legitimate family plans may be an option.

Consider the ROI. If a $20/month subscription saves you ten hours a month on research and studying, and your time is worth anything at all, the math works out. But be honest about whether you're saving time or just spending money to feel productive.

My Recommendations by Student Type

High school students: Start with ChatGPT Free and Perplexity Free. Add NotebookLM. That covers 90% of what you need.

Undergraduates in humanities/social sciences: Perplexity Free or Pro for research. Claude for writing and analysis. NotebookLM for readings. Semantic Scholar for finding papers.

Undergraduates in STEM: ChatGPT or Claude for general help. GitHub Copilot (free student access) for coding. Perplexity for research. NotebookLM for synthesizing readings.

Graduate students: Claude Pro or ChatGPT Plus for the higher limits you'll need. Perplexity Pro for research. Consensus for literature reviews. NotebookLM for document synthesis. Semantic Scholar for citation tracking.

A Warning About the Shiny New Thing

New AI tools launch constantly. Every week there's a new app claiming to revolutionize studying, note-taking, or research. Most are thin wrappers around the same underlying AI models, and most won't exist in a year.

Stick with established tools from companies likely to be around for a while. Your workflow should be built on stable foundations, not on the app trending on social media this week.

The tools in this chapter represent the current state of the art from companies with the resources and track record to maintain and improve them. Start here. Branch out only when you have a specific need these tools don't meet.

Now that you know what's available, let's talk about the most important topic in this entire book: how to use these tools without compromising your integrity.

Chapter 3: Academic Integrity and AI

The Chapter You Need to Read

This is the most important chapter in this book. Not because it's the most interesting — the practical chapters later are more fun — but because everything else depends on what you understand here. If you get the integrity framework right, every other chapter becomes more useful. If you get it wrong, nothing else in this book matters because you'll eventually face consequences that make the practical tips irrelevant.

I'm not going to lecture you. I'll give you a clear framework for thinking about AI and academic integrity, one that works across different schools, different policies, and different assignments. Then you get to decide how to apply it.

Why "Everyone Is Doing It" Isn't an Argument

Let's get this one out of the way first, because it's the most common justification students offer.

Yes, most of your classmates are using AI in some form. That's true. But "everyone is doing it" has never been a legitimate ethical argument for anything, and it doesn't start being one now. More importantly, it's not even accurate as applied to the specific behavior you might be considering. Most students are using AI to understand things better, not to generate submissions. The student who asks Claude to explain quantum superposition in simpler terms and the student who asks Claude to write their quantum mechanics problem set are both "using AI," but they're doing very different things.

When someone says "everyone is using it," they're conflating legitimate use with illegitimate use to justify the latter. Don't fall for this, even when you're telling it to yourself.

The Learning Test

Here's the simplest framework I can give you for determining whether a particular use of AI is appropriate:

After using AI, do you understand the material better than you did before?

If yes, you're probably using AI as a learning tool. If no, you're probably using AI as a bypass.

This is the Learning Test, and it's more reliable than any policy document because it gets at the actual purpose of education. Your school assigns work not because it wants to torture you but because the process of doing work is how learning happens. When AI helps you through that process, it's serving the same purpose as a tutor. When AI replaces that process, it's not.

Let's apply this to some concrete examples:

You're stuck on a calculus problem. You've worked on it for twenty minutes and don't know how to start. You type the problem into ChatGPT and ask it to solve step by step. Then you study the solution, identify where you went wrong, and work through two similar problems on your own. **Learning Test result: you understand the material better.** This is legitimate use.

You have ten calculus problems due tomorrow. You paste all ten into ChatGPT, copy the solutions, and submit them. You didn't look at the steps carefully. You couldn't solve a similar problem on your own. **Learning Test result: you don't understand the material any better.** This is cheating, regardless of whether your school's policy mentions AI.

You're writing a history essay. You brainstorm your thesis with Claude, asking it to challenge your argument and suggest counterpoints you hadn't considered. You write the essay yourself, incorporating the stronger argument you developed through that conversation. **Learning Test result: you understand the material better.** This is legitimate use.

You're writing a history essay. You give Claude your prompt and ask it to write the essay. You read through it, change a few words, and submit it. **Learning Test result: you don't understand the material any better.** This is plagiarism. It doesn't matter that an AI wrote it instead of another student.

The Learning Test isn't perfect — there are edge cases, and it doesn't override specific course policies that may be more restrictive. But it's the right starting point.

The Four Levels of AI Use

To think more precisely about where lines are, consider these four levels:

Level 1: AI as Reference

Using AI the way you'd use a textbook, encyclopedia, or knowledgeable friend. You ask it to explain something, clarify a concept, or provide background information. You then use your own understanding to do the actual work.

Examples: - "Explain the difference between monetary and fiscal policy in simple terms." - "What are the key themes in Toni Morrison's *Beloved*?" - "How does a binary search tree work?"

Integrity status: Almost universally acceptable. This is no different from reading a Wikipedia article or asking a classmate to explain something.

Level 2: AI as Tutor

Using AI interactively to work through a problem or develop understanding. This goes beyond reference — you're having a conversation, asking follow-up questions, and building comprehension through dialogue.

Examples: - "I got this calculus problem wrong. Here's my work. Where did I go wrong?" - "I'm trying to argue that Hamlet's hesitation is strategic, not psychological. What are the strongest counterarguments I need to address?" - "Walk me through how to approach designing a database schema for a library system."

Integrity status: Generally acceptable, and valuable. This is like having a patient tutor available 24/7. Some restrictive courses may limit this — check your syllabus.

Level 3: AI as Collaborator

Using AI to help produce parts of your work — generating outlines, drafting sections that you then substantially revise, editing your writing, or creating code that you modify and integrate. The final product is a real blend of your work and AI contribution.

Examples: - Having AI generate an outline for a paper that you then restructure and write. - Using AI to draft an introduction that you then rewrite in your own voice. - Generating code scaffolding that you then customize and debug. - Having AI edit your essay for clarity and argument structure.

Integrity status: This is the gray zone. Some courses allow this with disclosure. Others don't. You MUST check your course policy. If no policy exists, ask your professor. If you can't ask, err on the side of doing more yourself and disclosing what AI did.

Level 4: AI as Substitute

Submitting AI-generated work as your own with minimal modification. This is the scenario that every academic integrity policy is designed to prevent.

Examples: - Pasting an essay prompt into ChatGPT and submitting the output. - Having AI complete your problem set and copying the answers. - Using AI to write code that you don't understand and submitting it. - Having AI generate a lab report from your data without understanding the analysis.

Integrity status: This is cheating. Full stop. It doesn't matter what tools you used or how good the output is. If you didn't do the intellectual work, you're misrepresenting someone else's work as your own — the definition of academic dishonesty.

The Disclosure Principle

Here's a practical rule that will keep you safe in almost every situation:

If you would be uncomfortable telling your professor exactly how you used AI, you probably shouldn't have used it that way.

This is the disclosure principle. It doesn't mean you have to disclose every interaction — though many schools now require it — but it's a useful gut check. The student who used AI as a tutor has nothing to hide. The student who submitted AI-generated work has everything to hide.

Many courses now require explicit AI disclosure statements. Common formats include:

- A statement at the end of your submission describing what AI tools you used and how
- Submission of your AI conversation logs alongside your work
- A checkbox on the submission form indicating whether AI was used

If your course requires disclosure, be thorough and honest. Ironically, good disclosure of legitimate AI use often impresses professors — it shows sophistication and integrity.

Specific Scenarios and Where the Lines Are

Let me walk through common student scenarios and give you clear guidance:

Essays and Papers

Acceptable: Using AI to brainstorm thesis ideas, identify counterarguments, check your logic, improve your outline, and edit your draft for clarity. The key ideas, analysis, and writing voice must be yours.

Not acceptable: Having AI write sections you submit without substantially rewriting them. Even if you edit AI-generated text, if the core ideas and structure came from AI, it's not your work.

The bright line: Did you develop the argument, or did AI develop the argument? Your professor wants to see YOUR thinking, even if it's imperfect.

Problem Sets (Math, Science, Engineering)

Acceptable: Using AI to check your work, explain steps you don't understand, and help you learn the method so you can apply it yourself.

Not acceptable: Inputting problems and copying solutions without working through them independently.

The bright line: Can you solve a similar problem without AI? If yes, you learned. If no, you didn't.

Coding Assignments

Acceptable: Using AI to explain error messages, suggest debugging approaches, learn syntax for unfamiliar operations, and understand code examples.

Not acceptable: Generating complete solutions and submitting them. Even if you modify the code, if you can't explain every line and write similar code independently, you're misrepresenting your abilities.

The bright line: Can you explain your code line by line to your professor and write similar code from scratch? This is the standard.

Research Papers

Acceptable: Using AI to find sources, understand complex papers, generate search terms, identify gaps in literature, and organize your research.

Not acceptable: Using AI to write your literature review, generate your analysis, or synthesize findings that you haven't actually read and understood.

The bright line: Have you read the sources yourself? Do you understand the arguments? Can you discuss them in office hours? If not, AI did your research for you.

Group Projects

This gets complicated because different team members may have different understandings of what's appropriate. Establish AI use norms early. If AI helps coordinate or organize, that's generally fine. If AI does the work team members are responsible for, that's a problem for the whole group.

What Happens When You Get Caught

I'm including this not to scare you but because you should understand the stakes:

First offense at most universities: A formal warning, a zero on the assignment, or a grade reduction for the course. An academic integrity record is created that stays in your file.

Subsequent offenses: Course failure, suspension, or expulsion. Graduate students may lose funding, teaching positions, or advisor relationships.

Professional consequences: Medical schools, law schools, and other professional programs ask about academic integrity violations. Some licensing bodies do too. An integrity violation can follow you well beyond graduation.

The detection landscape: AI detection tools are unreliable, but that doesn't mean you won't get caught. Professors catch AI-generated work through means detection software can't replicate: they know your writing voice, they can tell when a student suddenly writes at a level inconsistent with their previous work, they ask follow-up questions in class or office hours, and they design assignments that are difficult to outsource to AI (specific to class discussions, based on personal experience, or requiring synthesis of multiple unique sources).

The Bigger Picture

Academic integrity isn't just about following rules. It's about what kind of professional — and what kind of person — you're becoming.

The doctor who cheated through medical school isn't prepared to treat patients. The engineer who used AI to pass structural analysis can't be trusted to design buildings. The lawyer who bypassed legal writing courses isn't ready to advocate for clients. These are extreme examples, but the principle applies everywhere: education is supposed to develop competence, and shortcuts that bypass that development create a gap between what you appear to know and what you actually know.

That gap always shows. Maybe not on the exam. Maybe not in the course. But eventually — in a job interview, in a professional situation, in a moment when you need to draw on knowledge you were supposed to have developed — the gap shows.

Using AI well means using it in ways that close gaps rather than hide them. It means being honest about what you know and what you don't. It means treating AI as a tool for growth, not a tool for deception.

Building Your Personal AI Ethics Framework

Here's what I'd recommend as a personal framework:

1. **Read the policy.** Every syllabus, every assignment, every course. Know the rules before you break them.

2. **Apply the Learning Test.** After every AI interaction, ask: do I understand this better now?

3. **Use the Disclosure Principle.** If you wouldn't tell your professor, don't do it.

4. **Stay at Levels 1 and 2 by default.** AI as Reference and AI as Tutor are safe in almost every context. Only move to Level 3 when the course explicitly permits it.

5. **When in doubt, ask.** Professors would almost always rather answer your question about AI use in advance than deal with an integrity case after the fact. Send the email. Ask in office hours. It takes thirty seconds and eliminates uncertainty.

6. **Document your process.** Keep your AI conversations. Save your prompts and outputs. If questions arise later, having documentation of your process — showing you used AI as a learning tool rather than a substitute — is powerful evidence.

7. **Develop independent competence.** Regularly test yourself without AI. Can you still do the work? If you've been using AI well, the answer should be yes, because AI has been helping you learn rather than doing the learning for you.

The Conversation with Yourself

The hardest part of academic integrity isn't the rules. It's the 2 AM moment when you're exhausted, the paper is due in six hours, you haven't started, and you know that AI could write something passable in ten minutes.

In that moment, no book will save you. No framework will override the pressure you feel. The decision is yours.

What I can tell you is this: the students who take the shortcut in that moment rarely do it just once. It becomes a pattern. And patterns become identities. The student who submits AI-generated work once finds it easier to do it again, and again, until the gap between their actual abilities and their transcripts becomes uncloseable.

The students who push through — who write the imperfect paper, submit the incomplete problem set, ask for the extension — come out the other side with something the shortcut-takers don't have: confidence that their abilities are real.

That confidence is worth more than any grade.

Now let's move on to the practical chapters — starting with how to use AI as the learning tool it's designed to be.

Part II: Learning and Studying

"The mind is not a vessel to be filled, but a fire to be kindled."

— Plutarch

Chapter 4: AI as a Learning Tool

The Tutor You Always Wanted

Remember the best teacher you ever had? The one who could tell when you were confused before you even asked a question? Who could explain the same concept five different ways until one of them clicked? Who had infinite patience and never made you feel stupid for not getting it?

AI can't replace that teacher. But it can do something that teacher couldn't: be available at 11 PM on a Sunday when you're stuck on thermodynamics and the assignment is due Monday morning.

This chapter is about using AI to learn — not to produce work, not to generate submissions, but to understand things you don't currently understand. When you use AI this way, you're doing what education is supposed to accomplish, just with a different kind of support.

The Socratic Method, Automated

The most effective way to use AI for learning is to have it ask YOU questions rather than simply give you answers. This is the Socratic method — the oldest teaching technique in the world — and AI does it surprisingly well when you set it up correctly.

Here's the difference:

The answer approach (less effective): > You: "What causes inflation?" > AI: "Inflation is caused by several factors including demand-pull inflation, cost-push inflation, and monetary policy..."

You read the answer. You feel like you understand. You move on. A week later, you can't explain inflation to save your life.

The Socratic approach (more effective): > You: "I need to understand what causes inflation for my econ midterm. Instead of just explaining it, can you quiz me first to see what I already know, then fill in the gaps? Ask me questions one at a time." > AI: "Sure. Let's start with the basics. If you had to explain inflation to a friend who knows nothing about economics, what would you say?" > You: "Prices going up?" > AI: "That's a good start – inflation is indeed a general increase in prices. But here's a deeper question: if the price of just one product goes up, like gasoline, is that inflation? Or does it need to be something broader?"

See the difference? In the second approach, you're actively thinking. You're retrieving what you know, identifying what you don't, and building connections. The research on learning is clear: active retrieval is far more effective than passive reading.

How to Set Up AI for Socratic Learning

The key is in your initial prompt. Here are templates that work:

The "Teach Me by Asking" Prompt

```
I'm studying [topic] for my [course name] class. I have an exam on [date].
Instead of explaining everything, I want you to:
1. Start by asking me what I already know about [topic]
2. Based on my answers, identify gaps in my understanding
3. Ask me questions that lead me to fill those gaps myself
4. Only explain directly if I'm really stuck after trying
5. Periodically check if I could now explain the concept to someone else
```

The "Challenge My Understanding" Prompt

```
I think I understand [concept], but I want to make sure. Ask me
progressively harder questions about it. Start basic and increase
difficulty. If I get something wrong, don't just tell me the right
answer – help me figure out where my reasoning went wrong.
```

The "Explain It Back" Prompt

```
I'm going to try to explain [concept] to you as if you're a classmate
who missed the lecture. After I explain, tell me:
- What I got right
- What I got wrong or oversimplified
- What important aspects I left out
- Follow-up questions that test whether I really understand or am just
  reciting
```

These approaches work because they force you to think rather than absorb passively. The AI becomes a practice partner, not a crutch.

Subject-Specific Learning Strategies

Learning with AI in Math

Math is where AI tutoring shines, because math understanding is built on sequential steps, and AI can identify exactly where your understanding breaks down.

Don't: "Solve this integral for me." **Do:** "I'm trying to integrate x^2 * e^x. I think I should use integration by parts, but I'm not sure how to choose u and dv. Can you help me think through the decision without just telling me?"

When you get a math problem wrong, try this approach:

```
Here's the problem: [problem]
Here's my work: [your attempt]
I got [your answer] but the correct answer is [correct answer].

Don't just show me the right solution. Instead:
1. Look at my work and find the exact step where I went wrong
2. Explain what mistake I made and why it's a common mistake
3. Give me a hint about how to fix it
4. Let me try again before showing the solution
```

This builds understanding because you're learning from your specific errors, not just memorizing a correct procedure.

Learning with AI in Sciences

Science courses combine conceptual understanding with quantitative problem-solving. AI can help with both:

For concepts:

```
I'm confused about [concept, e.g., "why entropy always increases"].
Can you give me three different analogies for this concept? Start
with a simple everyday analogy and progressively make them more
technically accurate.
```

Multiple analogies are powerful because different ones click for different people, and seeing several helps you understand what the analogies illustrate versus where they break down.

For lab work:

```
I ran an experiment measuring [what you measured]. My results show
[your data]. This doesn't match what I expected because [what you
expected and why]. Before I write my lab report, can you help me
think through possible reasons for the discrepancy? Don't just tell
me – ask me questions about my methodology that might reveal where
things went differently than expected.
```

Learning with AI in Humanities

Humanities courses emphasize interpretation, argumentation, and critical thinking — skills that AI can help you develop if you use it as a sparring partner rather than a ghostwriter.

For literary analysis:

```
I'm reading [text] and I need to develop an argument about [aspect].
I have a rough idea that [your initial thesis]. Instead of helping me
write about this, can you:
1. Tell me what's interesting about this argument
2. Tell me what's obvious or cliche about it
3. Suggest a way to make it more specific or surprising
4. Point me toward passages or details I should look at more carefully
```

For historical arguments:

```
I'm writing about [historical event/period]. My argument is [thesis].
Play devil's advocate: what are the three strongest counterarguments
to my position? For each one, suggest a primary source or type of
evidence I should look at to either address the counterargument or
refine my thesis.
```

Learning with AI in Languages

Language learning is one of the clearest wins for AI tutoring because the traditional bottleneck — lack of a conversation partner — is what AI solves.

```
I'm learning [language] at the [beginner/intermediate/advanced] level.
I want to practice conversational [language]. Please:
- Speak to me in [language]
- Keep your vocabulary at my level
- If I make a grammar or vocabulary mistake, gently correct me in
  brackets, then continue the conversation
```

```
- Periodically introduce one new vocabulary word in context
- Let's talk about [topic]
```

This gives you unlimited conversation practice with instant, non-judgmental correction — something hard to get even with a human tutor.

The Feynman Technique with AI

The Feynman Technique is one of the most effective learning strategies ever described: you try to explain a concept in simple terms, and wherever you get stuck, that's where you don't really understand it.

AI makes this technique practical by being a patient, knowledgeable audience:

```
I'm going to try to explain [concept] as simply as I can, as if
teaching it to a smart 12-year-old. After I'm done, I want you to:
1. Rate my explanation on accuracy (1-10)
2. Point out anything I said that was wrong or misleading
3. Identify the most important thing I left out
4. Ask me a question that tests whether I understand the WHY, not
   just the WHAT
```

This works because explaining forces retrieval and organization of knowledge, and the AI feedback catches errors and gaps you wouldn't notice yourself.

Debugging Your Understanding

One of the most powerful uses of AI is identifying and fixing misconceptions — the things you think you understand but don't.

```
I'm studying for my [subject] exam. I'm going to list what I think
are the key concepts and briefly explain each one. For each:
- If I'm right, just say "correct" and move on
- If I'm partly right, tell me what I'm missing
- If I'm wrong, ask me a question that helps me see why I'm wrong
  rather than just correcting me

Here are the concepts:
1. [Concept 1]: [Your understanding]
2. [Concept 2]: [Your understanding]
3. [Concept 3]: [Your understanding]
```

This is like a diagnostic exam, but interactive and immediate. It reveals what you know, what you don't, and — crucially — what you think you know but don't. That third category is the most dangerous on exams.

Making Connections Across Concepts

The difference between a B student and an A student often isn't knowledge of individual concepts — it's the ability to connect them. AI can help you build these connections:

```
I'm studying [Course] and we've covered [Concept A], [Concept B],
and [Concept C]. I understand each one individually, but I'm not sure
how they connect to each other. Can you:
1. Explain one way that [Concept A] relates to [Concept B]
2. Ask me if I can figure out how [Concept B] relates to [Concept C]
3. Help me see the bigger framework that all three fit into
```

This is especially valuable in courses that build cumulative understanding — where later topics depend on earlier ones and the final exam tests your ability to synthesize across the entire course.

When AI-Assisted Learning Isn't Working

Sometimes you'll have a conversation with AI and still feel confused. Here's how to diagnose why:

You're asking the wrong questions. If you can't articulate what you're confused about, AI can't help you. Try: "I don't understand [topic]. I can't even figure out what specifically I don't understand. Can you ask me some basic diagnostic questions to help us both figure out where I'm getting lost?"

You're going too fast. Slow down. Ask AI to break the concept into smaller pieces. "Can you explain just the first step of [process] and then wait for me to tell you when I'm ready for step two?"

You need a different modality. If textual explanations aren't working, try: "Can you explain this using an analogy?" or "Can you create a simple scenario or story that illustrates this concept?" or "Can you give me a worked example with specific numbers instead of abstract variables?"

You need the prerequisite. Sometimes you can't understand Concept B because you never really understood Concept A. "I'm stuck on [current topic]. What prerequisite knowledge do I need to understand this? Let's check whether I have those prerequisites first."

You need a human. AI is not a complete substitute for human instruction. If you're stuck after working with AI, go to office hours, visit the tutoring center, or form a study group. AI supplements human teaching — it doesn't replace it.

Building a Learning Habit

The students who get the most out of AI for learning don't just use it when they're stuck. They build it into their regular study routine:

After every lecture: Spend ten minutes asking AI to quiz you on what you just learned. This immediate retrieval practice sharply improves retention.

Before reading assignments: Ask AI to preview the key concepts you'll encounter. This creates a framework that makes the reading more comprehensible.

During study sessions: Alternate between studying independently and testing yourself with AI. The combination of reading/doing and AI-assisted retrieval practice is more effective than either alone.

Before exams: Use AI to create practice exams that match the format and difficulty of what you'll face. We'll cover this in detail in Chapter 7.

The Integrity Check

Everything in this chapter is about using AI to learn more — not to produce work for submission. The techniques here are designed to make you smarter, not to make your assignments easier. If you're applying the Learning Test from Chapter 3, every approach in this chapter should pass with flying colors: after using AI this way, you understand the material better than before.

That said, some professors may have policies that restrict even tutoring-style AI use. Read your syllabus. When in doubt, ask. And remember that the learning you gain from these techniques is yours — it lives in your head, not in a chat log. No policy can take away what you understand.

The next chapter builds on this foundation by showing you how to use AI for the task that causes students the most anxiety: research.

Chapter 5: Research with AI

The Research Problem

Research is where students lose the most time. Not because research itself is hard — though it can be — but because the process is inefficient. You start with a topic. You search databases and get either zero results or ten thousand. You read abstracts that don't tell you enough. You download papers you never finish. You chase rabbit holes that lead nowhere. You realize at 2 AM that you've been approaching the whole topic from the wrong angle.

AI doesn't eliminate these problems, but it changes the efficiency of the research process. It helps you find sources faster, understand them more quickly, spot gaps in your coverage, and synthesize findings across multiple papers. Used well, it turns a thirty-hour research process into a ten-hour one — and produces better results.

Used poorly, it gives you fabricated citations and false confidence. So let's talk about doing it well.

The Cardinal Rule of AI Research

Before we go any further: **never cite a source you found through AI without independently verifying that it exists and says what AI claims it says.**

This rule is non-negotiable. Here's why: general-purpose AI models (ChatGPT, Claude, Gemini) sometimes fabricate citations. They'll give you a plausible-sounding author name, journal title, year, and even DOI — and none of it will be real. This isn't a bug that got fixed in 2024. It still happens in 2026, especially on less-known topics.

The tools I'll recommend in this chapter — Perplexity, Consensus, Semantic Scholar, Google Scholar — are less prone to this because they search actual databases rather than generating text. But even with these tools, verify everything. Click the link. Read at least the abstract. Confirm the source actually supports the claim you're using it for.

A fabricated citation in a submitted paper isn't just a mistake — it's evidence that you didn't do the research, and professors know it.

Phase 1: Topic Exploration and Scoping

Before you dive into databases, you need to map your topic landscape. This is where general-purpose AI excels.

Getting Oriented

When you're starting research on an unfamiliar topic, use AI to build a mental map:

```
I'm writing a research paper on [topic] for my [course name] class.
The paper needs to be [length] and use [number] scholarly sources.

Before I start searching for sources, help me understand the landscape:
1. What are the 3-4 major subtopics or debates within this topic?
2. What are the key terms I should be searching for in databases?
3. What disciplines study this topic? (So I know which databases to use)
4. Are there any landmark studies or papers I should definitely know about?
5. What's the current state of the field — is this a settled topic or an
   active area of debate?
```

This gives you a map before you start driving. Instead of searching blindly, you know what you're looking for and where to look.

Narrowing Your Focus

A common research problem is a topic that's too broad. AI can help you narrow:

```
My paper is on [broad topic]. I need to narrow this to something I can
cover in [length]. Here are the aspects I find most interesting:
[your interests]

Suggest 3-4 specific, arguable thesis statements I could pursue. For
each one, tell me:
- Whether there's enough scholarly literature to support a paper
- What the main counterargument would be
- How controversial or original it is
```

Notice that you're not asking AI to pick your thesis — you're asking it to help you evaluate options so YOU can make an informed choice.

Phase 2: Finding Sources

This is where you need the right tools, not just the right prompts.

The Source-Finding Stack

Use these tools in this order:

Step 1: Perplexity for initial discovery. Search your topic on Perplexity to find key sources, major authors, and the contours of the scholarly conversation. Perplexity searches the web in real time and provides numbered citations — a good starting point.

```
[In Perplexity]
What does the peer-reviewed research say about [your specific thesis/question]?
Focus on studies published in the last 5-10 years. I need academic sources,
not news articles or blog posts.
```

Step 2: Google Scholar for depth. Take the key terms, author names, and paper titles from your Perplexity results and search them on Google Scholar. Use Google Scholar's features: - "Cited by" links to find newer papers that build on a key study - "Related articles" to find similar work - Date filters to focus on recent research - Author profiles to find other work by key researchers

Step 3: Semantic Scholar for citation mapping. Search your key papers on Semantic Scholar to understand the citation network — who cites whom, which papers are the most influential, and how the scholarly conversation has evolved.

Step 4: Consensus for specific claims. When you need evidence for a specific claim in your paper, use Consensus to search for peer-reviewed studies that support or refute it.

Step 5: Your school's databases. JSTOR, PubMed, IEEE Xplore, PsycINFO, Web of Science — your library gives you access to databases that Perplexity and Google Scholar can find but can't always open in full text. Use the sources you've identified to pull full papers through your library's subscriptions.

Building a Search Strategy

AI can help you build more effective database searches:

```
I'm searching for sources on [topic] in [database name]. My initial
search for "[your search terms]" returned [too many/too few] results.

Help me:
1. Suggest better search terms, including synonyms and related concepts
2. Recommend Boolean operators to narrow or broaden my search
3. Suggest MeSH terms or subject headings if applicable
4. Identify adjacent fields where relevant research might be published
   under different terminology
```

This pays off in fields where jargon varies — the same concept might be called "cognitive load" in education research, "working memory demands" in psychology, and "information processing burden" in HCI.

Phase 3: Understanding What You Find

Finding sources is half the battle. Understanding them — especially dense academic papers — is where many students struggle.

Reading Dense Papers with AI

Upload a PDF to Claude or ChatGPT and use prompts like:

```
I've uploaded a research paper. Please help me understand it by:
1. Summarizing the main research question in one sentence
2. Describing the methodology in plain language
3. Listing the 3-4 key findings
4. Explaining the limitations the authors acknowledge
5. Telling me how this paper relates to [your research topic]

Important: I need to understand this paper well enough to discuss it
in my own paper, so don't oversimplify. But do translate jargon into
language I can follow.
```

For Statistics-Heavy Papers

```
This paper uses [statistical method]. I understand the basics of
statistics but I'm not sure how to interpret:
- [specific result, e.g., "the interaction effect in Table 3"]
- [specific result]

Explain what these results mean in the context of the paper's argument.
What do the p-values, effect sizes, and confidence intervals tell us
about how confident we should be in the findings?
```

For Theoretical Papers

```
This paper presents a theoretical framework about [topic]. I'm having
trouble understanding:
- How this framework differs from [other framework you know]
- What the practical implications of this theory are
- Whether this is a widely accepted framework or a contested one

Help me understand this, but also help me think critically about it.
What are the potential weaknesses of this framework?
```

Building a Literature Matrix

As you read multiple papers, tracking how they relate to each other becomes its own challenge. AI can help:

```
I've read the following papers for my literature review:
1. [Author, Year]: [Brief summary of findings]
2. [Author, Year]: [Brief summary of findings]
3. [Author, Year]: [Brief summary of findings]
[etc.]

Help me:
1. Identify themes across these papers – what do multiple papers agree on?
2. Identify contradictions – where do papers disagree?
3. Identify gaps – what questions do these papers leave unanswered?
4. Suggest how to organize these into a coherent literature review
   (thematically, chronologically, or by methodology?)
```

This is one of the most valuable things AI can do for research. Seeing patterns across multiple sources is hard for humans (we process papers one at a time), but AI can hold all the papers in context at once and surface connections you might miss.

Phase 4: Research Synthesis

Once you've found and understood your sources, you need to synthesize them into a coherent argument. This is the intellectual core of research writing, and it's where AI assists rather than leads.

Developing Your Argument

```
Based on the sources I've described, I'm developing this argument:
[your thesis]

Play critic:
1. Is this thesis supported by the evidence I've found?
2. Which of my sources most strongly support it?
3. Which sources contradict it or complicate it?
4. What additional evidence would make this argument stronger?
5. Is there an obvious counterargument I need to address?
```

Organizing Your Paper

```
I have [number] sources and my thesis is [thesis]. Help me think through
the structure of my paper:
1. What's the most logical order to present my evidence?
2. Should I organize by theme, by chronology, or by methodology?
3. Where should I address counterarguments?
4. What transitions between sections would make the argument flow?

Don't write the paper – just help me plan the structure.
```

Note that last line: "Don't write the paper." This keeps you in the driver's seat. AI helps you think through the architecture; you do the building.

Common Research Mistakes to Avoid

The Echo Chamber

AI often finds sources that support whatever position you're investigating. This feels good but produces weak papers. Ask explicitly for counterevidence:

```
My thesis is [thesis]. I've found plenty of supporting evidence.
Now find me the strongest arguments and evidence AGAINST my position.
I need to address these in my paper.
```

The Recency Bias

AI tools lean toward recent sources. For many topics, foundational older works are essential. Ask specifically:

```
What are the seminal/foundational papers on [topic]? I'm looking for
the works that established this field or changed how researchers
think about it, even if they're decades old.
```

The Breadth Without Depth Trap

AI makes it easy to find many sources fast, which leads to a paper that references twenty papers but engages deeply with none of them. Your professor can tell the difference between a student who read five papers carefully and a student who skimmed twenty.

Quality over quantity. Read fewer papers more carefully. Use AI to help you understand each one deeply rather than to accumulate a long bibliography.

Trusting AI Summaries as Substitutes for Reading

When AI summarizes a paper, that summary is filtered through the AI's understanding, which may miss nuance, misread emphasis, or flatten complexity. AI summaries are starting points, not endpoints.

Always read the key sections yourself: the abstract, introduction, methodology, key results tables, and conclusion. Use AI summaries to help you parse what you're reading, not to replace the reading.

NotebookLM: Your Research Hub

Google's NotebookLM deserves special mention because it's built for the kind of work I'm describing in this chapter.

Upload your research papers, lecture notes, and course materials. Then ask questions that only reference your uploaded sources. Because NotebookLM works exclusively with the documents you provide, it doesn't hallucinate sources or fabricate citations — it can only reference what you've given it.

For synthesizing across papers:

```
Looking at all the papers I've uploaded, what are the main areas of
agreement and disagreement on [topic]?
```

For finding specific evidence:

```
Which of my sources provides evidence about [specific claim]? Quote
the relevant passages.
```

For study preparation:

```
Based on all my research materials, create a comprehensive overview
of the current state of knowledge on [topic]. Note where evidence is
strong and where it's contested.
```

The Integrity Dimension of AI-Assisted Research

Research is the academic activity where AI use is most broadly accepted, because finding and understanding sources is plainly a learning support activity. But there are still lines:

Acceptable: Using AI to find sources, understand papers, identify connections, organize your research, and build a search strategy.

Gray area: Having AI draft a literature review outline that you then write. Having AI suggest how to frame your argument. Using AI to identify which quotes to use.

Not acceptable: Having AI write your literature review. Citing sources you haven't read. Using AI-generated analysis as your own interpretation. Presenting AI's synthesis as your original contribution.

The line is: AI can help you do research better, but the intellectual work of analyzing, interpreting, and arguing must be yours. Your professor is evaluating your ability to engage with sources, not AI's ability to summarize them.

Putting It All Together

Here's a complete AI-assisted research workflow:

1. **Explore** the topic landscape with a general-purpose AI
2. **Search** for sources using Perplexity, Google Scholar, Semantic Scholar, and your school's databases
3. **Read** papers yourself, using AI to help you understand dense or technical sections
4. **Track** your sources in a literature matrix, using AI to identify patterns
5. **Develop** your argument by stress-testing it with AI
6. **Organize** your paper structure with AI assistance
7. **Write** the paper yourself (more on this in the next chapter)

8. **Verify** every citation independently before submission

This process produces better research than either purely manual or purely AI-driven work. You're using AI to amplify your capabilities, not replace them. The understanding you develop is real, the sources are verified, and the argument is yours.

That's research done right.

Chapter 6: Writing Better Papers

The Goal Isn't a Better Paper — It's a Better Writer

Here's the uncomfortable truth about AI and writing: AI can produce a decent paper faster than you can. It generates coherent paragraphs, constructs logical arguments, transitions smoothly between ideas, and does it all in thirty seconds. If you measure success by the quality of a single paper, AI wins.

But that's the wrong measurement. You're not in school to produce one paper. You're in school to become someone who can produce papers — and emails, reports, briefs, analyses, proposals, and every other form of professional writing — for the rest of your career. AI can help you become that person, or it can prevent you from becoming that person. The difference is entirely in how you use it.

This chapter is about using AI to write better — not to write less.

What AI Is Actually Good At in Writing

Start by understanding where AI genuinely helps, so you apply it to those areas and don't lean on it where you shouldn't.

Brainstorming. AI is excellent at generating ideas you haven't considered. It can produce fifteen potential thesis statements in a minute, suggest angles on a topic you hadn't thought of, and surface arguments that need addressing. This is pure value — more raw material for your brain to work with.

Outlining. AI helps you organize your ideas into a logical structure. It can suggest where to put your strongest argument, how to build toward your conclusion, and what order makes the most sense for a reader.

Overcoming the blank page. The hardest sentence to write is the first one. AI can help you start — not by writing your introduction, but by helping you talk through what you want to say until you find your opening.

Revision and feedback. AI is a tireless, patient editor. It catches weak arguments, unclear sentences, missing transitions, and logical gaps. This is where AI adds the most value to student writing.

Style and clarity. AI helps you write more clearly, cut wordiness, vary your sentence structure, and adjust tone for different audiences.

Grammar and mechanics. The least interesting but most reliable AI contribution. Every AI tool catches grammar, spelling, and punctuation errors.

What AI Is Bad At in Writing

Your voice. AI doesn't know what you sound like. It can mimic generic academic writing, but it can't replicate the specific way you think and argue. Your voice is valuable — it's what makes your paper different from the ten thousand other papers on the same topic.

Your ideas. AI can rearrange and refine ideas, but the truly original insight — the connection nobody else made, the reading that challenges conventional interpretation, the argument that comes from your specific experience and knowledge — has to come from you.

Deep analysis. AI can summarize what others have said. It struggles with new analysis — reading between lines, challenging assumptions, building novel theoretical frameworks. This is exactly the skill your professor is trying to develop in you.

Understanding your assignment. AI doesn't know your professor, your course, what was discussed in class, what angle your professor wants, or what separates an A paper from a B paper in this specific context. You do. That contextual knowledge is irreplaceable.

The AI-Assisted Writing Process

Here's a writing workflow that uses AI at every stage without losing your voice or your learning:

Stage 1: Thinking Before Writing

Before you write anything, think. AI can help with this:

```
I need to write a [length] paper on [topic] for my [course] class.
The assignment asks me to [specific requirements].

Here are my initial thoughts: [your raw ideas, even if messy]

Help me think through this by:
1. What's the strongest argument I could make from these ideas?
2. What am I missing?
3. What would a skeptical reader object to?
4. What evidence would I need to make this argument convincing?
```

You're thinking out loud with AI as a sounding board. The ideas are yours; AI pressure-tests and develops them.

Stage 2: Building an Outline

```
Based on our discussion, here's my thesis: [your thesis]

Help me build an outline for a [length] paper. For each section, suggest:
- The main point of the section
- What evidence or examples should go there
- How it connects to the section before and after it

I want [number] body paragraphs/sections.
```

Review the outline critically. Move things around. Add your own ideas. Cut sections that don't serve your argument. The outline should feel like yours by the time you start writing.

Stage 3: Writing the Draft — Yourself

This is the part where you close the AI tab and write. Yes, really.

The draft is where your voice develops, where your ideas take shape in your own words, where you discover what you actually think about the topic. If AI writes this part, you've skipped the most valuable stage of the process.

Your draft will be messy. It will have awkward sentences, unclear transitions, and paragraphs that don't quite work. That's normal. That's what drafts are for.

Write the whole thing. Then bring AI back in.

Stage 4: AI-Assisted Revision

This is where AI provides the most value per dollar. You've done the thinking and the writing. Now use AI to make it better:

For argument strength:

```
Here's my paper. Read it as a critical but fair professor. Tell me:
1. Is my thesis clear?
2. Does each paragraph support my thesis?
3. Are there logical gaps in my argument?
4. Where is my evidence weakest?
5. What's the strongest counterargument I haven't addressed?
```

For clarity:

```
Read my paper for clarity. Identify:
1. Sentences that are confusing or could be misread
2. Paragraphs where I make a point but don't clearly explain it
3. Jargon I use without defining
4. Places where I assume knowledge the reader might not have
```

For structure:

```
Look at the organization of my paper. Tell me:
1. Does the order of paragraphs make logical sense?
2. Are there better places for any of my points?
3. Do my transitions connect ideas or just signal a new paragraph?
4. Does my conclusion follow from the argument, or does it introduce
   new ideas that should have been in the body?
```

For style:

```
Review my writing style:
1. Point out sentences that are unnecessarily wordy
2. Find places where I use passive voice when active would be stronger
3. Identify repetitive phrasing or words I overuse
4. Suggest where I could vary my sentence length and structure
```

Stage 5: Targeted Rewriting

After getting AI feedback, rewrite problem areas yourself. Here's a technique for when you're stuck on a specific sentence or paragraph:

```
I'm trying to say [explain your idea in casual language]. Here are
three attempts I've made:

1. [attempt 1]
2. [attempt 2]
3. [attempt 3]

None of these feel right. Can you suggest three alternative ways to
express this idea? I'll use them as inspiration but will write the
final version in my own words.
```

This preserves your ownership of the writing while giving you models to learn from. Over time, exposure to different ways of expressing ideas sharpens your own writing instincts.

Stage 6: Final Polish

Use AI for a final pass on mechanics:

```
Proofread my paper for:
- Grammar and punctuation errors
- Spelling mistakes
- Formatting inconsistencies
- Citation format errors (I'm using [APA/MLA/Chicago])
- Any remaining unclear sentences
```

Writing at Different Academic Levels

High School Papers

Your teachers are developing your ability to form and defend arguments. AI can help by: - Showing you what a strong thesis statement looks like versus a weak one - Helping you find evidence for claims you've made - Pointing out where your argument is unclear

But the writing itself — even when imperfect — needs to be yours. Your teachers are tracking your writing development, and they know what you sound like.

Undergraduate Papers

In college, expectations for argumentation and evidence rise sharply. AI is most valuable for: - Helping you develop more sophisticated arguments (moving from "I think X" to "The evidence suggests X because...") - Reviewing your use of evidence (are you analyzing sources or just quoting them?) - Sharpening your academic register without making you sound like a textbook

Graduate-Level Writing

At the graduate level, you're expected to contribute original analysis to scholarly conversations. AI can: - Help you position your argument within the existing literature - Spot logical gaps in complex arguments - Review your methodology discussions for clarity - Help you manage the relationship between your literature review and your original contribution

Chapter 13 goes deeper into graduate writing specifically.

Specific Types of Academic Writing

The Argumentative Essay

The core of most undergraduate writing. Key AI uses: - Stress-testing your thesis before you write - Identifying the strongest opposing arguments - Reviewing your conclusion to ensure it follows from your evidence

The line: AI can help you develop a better argument. It shouldn't generate the argument for you.

The Research Paper

Covered extensively in Chapter 5. For the writing stage: - Use AI to check that your paper structure matches conventions in your field - Have AI review whether you're properly integrating sources (analyzing vs. summarizing) - Check that your citations are formatted correctly

The Lab Report

Lab reports follow strict conventions that AI knows well: - Use AI to check your report against the standard structure (abstract, intro, methods, results, discussion, conclusion) - Have AI review your discussion section for logical connections between your results and your hypothesis - Ask AI if your methods section is detailed enough to replicate

The line: Your data, observations, and analysis must be entirely your own. AI can help you communicate them more clearly.

The Literature Review

The most research-intensive form of academic writing: - Use AI to help organize themes across sources (see Chapter 5) - Have AI check whether you're synthesizing or merely summarizing - Ask AI if there are obvious gaps in your coverage

The line: You must have read the sources yourself. AI-generated literature reviews that you haven't verified against the original papers are academic fraud.

The Reflection or Response Paper

These are personal and analytical — and ironically, the type of writing where AI is least helpful and most detectable. Your professor wants YOUR reaction. AI doesn't have reactions to your experiences.

Best use of AI here: after writing your draft, ask AI whether your reflection demonstrates genuine critical thinking or stays superficial.

Common Writing Mistakes AI Can Help You Fix

The "so what?" problem. You make a point but don't explain why it matters. Ask AI: "After reading my paper, what's the 'so what' — why should a reader care about this argument?"

The evidence dump. You quote or cite sources but don't analyze them. Ask AI: "Identify places where I present evidence but don't explain what it means or how it supports my argument."

The wandering paragraph. Each paragraph should make one point. Ask AI: "For each paragraph, can you identify the single main point? If you can't, that paragraph needs work."

The weak introduction. Your intro should state your thesis and roadmap your argument, not provide dictionary definitions or overly broad generalizations. Ask AI: "Does my introduction tell the reader exactly what I'm going to argue and how?"

The anticlimactic conclusion. Your conclusion should synthesize, not summarize. Ask AI: "Does my conclusion add anything beyond restating what I already said in the body?"

Developing Your Writing Over Time

The long game of AI-assisted writing is that you gradually need AI less. Here's how that progression works:

Semester 1: You rely on AI for brainstorming, outlining, and heavy revision. You're learning what good academic writing looks like by seeing how AI suggests improvements to your drafts.

Semester 2: You need less help with structure and clarity because you've internalized those patterns. You still use AI for argument testing and final revision.

Semester 3 and beyond: You use AI mainly for feedback on specific weaknesses and for catching errors you tend to make. Your voice is established, your argument construction is solid, and AI is a polish tool, not a crutch.

If you rely on AI more over time rather than less, something is wrong. The trajectory should always be toward independence.

The Voice Question

A common concern about AI-assisted writing is losing your voice. Here's how to prevent that:

Never let AI write your first draft. Your voice lives in your first draft. It's raw and imperfect, but it's yours.

When AI suggests revisions, don't just accept them. Read the suggestion, understand why it's better, then write your own version that incorporates the improvement in your own way.

Periodically write without any AI assistance. Treat it like a musician practicing without a metronome — make sure you can still perform on your own.

Read your final paper aloud. If it doesn't sound like something you'd say, you've let AI override your voice. Revise until it sounds like a more polished version of how you naturally communicate.

Your voice isn't a liability. It's an asset. The best academic writing is clear, precise, and distinctly authored. AI helps you achieve clarity and precision; you maintain the distinctiveness.

The Bottom Line

AI should make your writing process more effective, not easier. The best papers still require hard thinking, careful research, multiple drafts, and genuine engagement with your topic. AI accelerates each of those stages without skipping any of them.

The student who uses AI to become a better writer graduates with a skill that compounds for an entire career. The student who uses AI to bypass writing graduates with a degree and no skills — and that gap becomes painfully obvious in the first year of professional life.

Write your papers. Use AI to make them better. And over time, watch yourself become the kind of writer who needs AI less and less.

Chapter 7: Studying and Exam Prep

Why Most Studying Doesn't Work

Hard truth: most study techniques students use are inefficient. Rereading notes, highlighting textbooks, passively reviewing slides — research on learning consistently shows these methods feel productive but produce poor retention. You recognize the material when you see it, which tricks you into thinking you know it. Then the exam arrives and you can't recall it without the visual cue.

The techniques that actually work — active recall, spaced repetition, interleaving, elaborative interrogation — are harder. They demand more effort. They feel less productive in the moment, even though they produce dramatically better results.

This is where AI becomes transformative. Not because it makes studying easier — though it does — but because it makes the most effective study techniques accessible and practical. AI can quiz you, generate practice problems, space your review, and test your understanding in ways passive study can't.

Active Recall with AI

Active recall means testing yourself on material rather than simply reviewing it. Decades of cognitive science research show that retrieving information from memory strengthens that memory far more effectively than re-reading or re-listening.

AI is a near-perfect active recall partner because it generates unlimited questions at any difficulty level.

The Basic Quiz Approach

```
I have an exam on [topic/course] covering [list of topics/chapters].
Quiz me with a mix of question types:
- Multiple choice (4 options)
- Short answer
- "Explain the concept" questions
- Application questions (give me a scenario and ask me to apply the concept)

Start with medium difficulty. If I get several right, increase difficulty.
```

```
If I struggle, ease up and ask simpler questions to rebuild my foundation.

Ask one question at a time. After I answer, tell me if I'm right or wrong
and briefly explain why. Then move to the next question.
```

This beats reading through your notes because every question forces you to retrieve information, which strengthens the memory trace.

The Misconception Hunter

```
I'm studying [topic] and I want to make sure I don't have any
misconceptions. Ask me questions that target common misunderstandings
in this topic. These should be questions where the intuitive answer
is wrong – where students typically make mistakes.

After each question, explain why the common wrong answer is wrong and
why the correct answer is correct.
```

This technique targets the material most likely to trip you up on an exam.

The "Teach It Back" Quiz

```
Give me a concept from [topic list]. I'll try to explain it as if I'm
teaching it to someone who knows nothing about the subject. After my
explanation, rate it:
- Accuracy (did I get anything wrong?)
- Completeness (did I leave out anything important?)
- Clarity (would a beginner understand my explanation?)

Then give me the next concept.
```

If you can explain something clearly and accurately, you understand it. If you can't, you've found a gap.

Spaced Repetition

Spaced repetition is the most efficient study technique known to cognitive science. Instead of cramming the night before, you review material at increasing intervals — first a day later, then three days, then a week, then two weeks. Each review strengthens the memory just as it's about to fade.

Building Spaced Repetition with AI

```
I have an exam in [number] days covering [topics]. Help me create a
study schedule using spaced repetition:
1. List the key concepts I need to know
2. Prioritize them by difficulty and importance
3. Create a day-by-day review schedule where I review each concept
   at increasing intervals
4. For each study session, create 5-10 practice questions on the
   concepts scheduled for that day
```

Creating Flashcard Content

While dedicated flashcard apps (Anki, Quizlet) are great for spaced repetition, AI can generate the content for them:

```
I need flashcards for [topic]. For each concept, create:
- Front of card: A question or prompt
- Back of card: A concise, accurate answer

Make sure the questions require recall, not recognition. Don't make
the front of the card a fill-in-the-blank of the answer – ask
questions that require me to actually understand the concept.

Create [number] flashcards covering [specific topics].
```

Important: Review the flashcards AI generates. Check them against your notes and textbook. AI occasionally gets details wrong, and studying wrong flashcards is worse than not studying at all.

Exam-Specific Preparation

Practice Exams

```
Create a practice exam for [course] covering [topics]. The real exam
will be [format: multiple choice / short answer / essay / mixed].
It will have approximately [number] questions and last [duration].

Make the difficulty level [match my professor's exams / slightly harder
than typical exams / focus on conceptual understanding].

Include an answer key with explanations, but put it at the end so I
can take the full exam first without peeking.
```

After taking the practice exam, review not just what you got wrong, but why:

```
Here are my answers to the practice exam: [your answers]

For each question I got wrong:
1. Explain why my answer was incorrect
2. Explain what misconception or knowledge gap led to my error
3. Suggest what I should review to prevent this type of error
4. Give me one similar practice question to try now
```

Predicting Exam Questions

Your professor emphasizes certain topics in lecture, spends more time on some concepts than others, and has patterns in how they write exams. AI helps you think strategically:

```
I'm studying for my [course] exam. Here's what my professor emphasized
in lecture: [key topics, concepts they spent the most time on, things
they said were important].

Here's what was covered but not emphasized: [peripheral topics].

Based on what professors typically emphasize and test, what are the
most likely exam questions? Generate 10 questions that are most likely
to appear, and explain why each one is likely.
```

This isn't cheating — it's strategic studying. Every experienced student learns to predict exam questions by tracking what professors emphasize.

Preparing for Different Exam Formats

Multiple choice:

```
Generate [number] multiple-choice questions on [topic]. For each question:
- Make one answer clearly correct
- Make one answer almost correct but wrong for a specific reason
- Make one answer a common misconception
- Make one answer clearly wrong

After I answer, explain why the correct answer is correct AND why
each wrong answer is wrong.
```

Short answer:

```
Give me [number] short answer questions on [topic]. For each, tell me:
- What a perfect answer includes (key points to hit)
- What a common incomplete answer looks like
- How many points I'd lose for missing each key element

I'll practice writing answers, then you compare mine to the ideal.
```

Essay exams:

```
Give me [number] essay prompts on [topic] that a professor might use
on an exam. For each prompt:
1. What is the prompt really asking? (Sometimes essay prompts test
   specific skills – argument, analysis, synthesis, comparison)
2. What are the key points a strong answer must address?
3. What's the most common mistake students make on this type of question?
4. Write a brief outline of what an A-grade response would cover
```

Problem-solving exams (math, science, engineering):

```
Generate [number] problems similar to what I'll see on my [course] exam.
Vary the difficulty. For each problem:
- State the problem
- After I attempt it, check my work step by step
- Identify where I went right and where I went wrong
- If I got it right, give me a harder variation
- If I got it wrong, explain the concept I need to review
```

Concept Mapping

Understanding how concepts relate is often the difference between a student who knows the material and a student who performs well on exams. AI helps you build those connections:

```
Here are the main topics from my [course]:
[list of topics]

Help me understand how they connect:
1. Which concepts are prerequisites for others?
2. Which concepts are related but distinct (and how)?
3. Which concepts show up in multiple topics?
4. If I understand [Concept A], how does that help me understand
   [Concept B]?
```

This pays off for cumulative finals, where you need to see the course as a coherent whole rather than a collection of isolated topics.

Study Plans

The Pre-Exam Study Plan

```
I have [number] days until my [course] exam. The exam covers [topics].

Here's my honest self-assessment of each topic:
- [Topic 1]: [strong / moderate / weak]
- [Topic 2]: [strong / moderate / weak]
- [Topic 3]: [strong / moderate / weak]
[etc.]

I can study approximately [hours] per day.

Create a study plan that:
1. Allocates more time to my weak areas
2. Doesn't neglect strong areas (quick review to maintain)
3. Includes practice problems, not just review
4. Builds in breaks (I know they're important)
5. Schedules the hardest material when I'm freshest (mornings / evenings)
6. Includes a final review day before the exam
```

The Semester-Long Study Strategy

```
I'm taking [course] this semester. The major assessments are:
[list of exams, papers, projects with dates]

Help me create a semester-long study strategy where I review material
regularly rather than cramming before each exam. I want to use spaced
repetition principles – reviewing material at increasing intervals
after it's first taught.

I have approximately [hours] per week available for this course
outside of class.
```

Subject-Specific Study Strategies

Studying for Science Exams

```
For my [biology/chemistry/physics] exam, I need to study both
concepts and problem-solving. Create a study session structure:
1. Start with concept review (quiz me on key principles)
2. Move to problem-solving practice (start easy, increase difficulty)
```

```
3. End with integration questions (problems that combine multiple concepts)
Each session should be about [duration].
```

Studying for History/Social Science Exams

```
For my [history/political science/sociology] exam, I need to:
1. Know key events, dates, and figures
2. Understand cause-and-effect relationships
3. Be able to construct arguments using historical evidence
4. Compare and contrast different periods/movements/theories

Create a study session that covers all four areas. Start with factual
recall, then move to analysis and argumentation practice.
```

Studying for Math Exams

```
For my [math course] exam covering [topics], I need practice problems
organized by difficulty:
1. Basic application (can I use the formula/technique?)
2. Intermediate (can I choose the right technique for the problem?)
3. Advanced (can I combine techniques and handle unusual cases?)

For each difficulty level, give me [number] problems. After I work
through them, identify patterns in my errors.
```

Studying for Language Exams

```
For my [language] exam, I need to practice:
- Vocabulary: Quiz me on the vocabulary from chapters [X-Y]
- Grammar: Give me sentences to translate that test [specific grammar concepts]
- Reading comprehension: Give me a paragraph in [language] and ask
  questions about it
- Writing: Give me a prompt and evaluate my response for grammar,
  vocabulary, and coherence
```

What AI Can't Do for Exam Prep

AI can't replace sleep. Studying all night with AI is still studying all night, and sleep deprivation destroys exam performance more reliably than poor studying. Get sleep.

AI can't replace consistent effort. A week of AI-assisted studying can't compensate for a semester of not attending class. AI works best when it reinforces material you've been engaging with all along.

AI can't guarantee accuracy. AI occasionally generates wrong practice questions or wrong answers. Always cross-reference with your course materials — your textbook and lecture notes are the authoritative sources, not AI.

AI can't replicate exam conditions. When you take a practice exam, simulate real conditions: no notes, no AI, timed, at a desk. The point of a practice exam is to experience the conditions you'll face, including the pressure.

The Night Before the Exam

```
Tomorrow is my [course] exam. I've been studying for [number] days.
Here are the topics I feel confident about: [list]
Here are the topics I'm still worried about: [list]

I have [number] hours tonight. Help me use them effectively:
1. For my weak areas: give me a focused review of the most important
   concepts (not everything – just the highest-value material)
2. For my strong areas: give me 2-3 quick questions to confirm I still
   have them
3. Tell me what to focus on and what to let go – I can't learn
   everything tonight
```

That last point matters. AI helps you triage. If you're out of time, it's better to know six topics solidly than to have a shallow grasp of all ten.

After the Exam

The learning doesn't stop when you hand in the exam:

```
I just took my [course] exam. Here are the questions I remember
struggling with: [describe them]

For each one:
1. Walk me through the correct approach
2. Explain what I probably did wrong
3. Tell me what concept I need to solidify before the next exam

I want to actually learn from my mistakes, not just forget about them.
```

This is one of the most underused study techniques: post-exam reflection. Most students get their grade and move on. The students who review their mistakes — understanding not just what the right answer was but why they got it wrong — improve steadily throughout the semester.

Building Study Skills That Last

The study techniques in this chapter aren't just exam hacks. Active recall, spaced repetition, interleaving, and self-testing are skills that transfer to professional life. The doctor who can recall drug interactions, the lawyer who can recall precedents, the engineer who can recall design principles — all rely on the same cognitive mechanisms you're training now.

AI makes these techniques practical by removing the setup burden. You no longer spend an hour writing practice questions — AI does that in seconds. You spend your time on what actually builds knowledge: struggling with the material, making mistakes, and correcting them.

Study smarter. Use AI to make the best techniques accessible. And get some sleep.

Part III: AI Across Disciplines

"Study hard what interests you the most in the most undisciplined, irreverent and original manner possible."

— Richard Feynman

Chapter 8: Math and Science with AI

The Double-Edged Sword

Math and science are where AI's capabilities and risks are both sharpest. AI can solve equations, generate proofs, explain complex phenomena, analyze data, and debug lab results — often in seconds. For a struggling student, that power is intoxicating. The problem set that would take three hours of frustration can be done in minutes.

Which is exactly why this chapter starts with a warning: if you use AI to get answers in math and science, you will fail. Not morally — practically. Math and science courses are cumulative. Chapter 3 builds on Chapter 2, which builds on Chapter 1. If AI does Chapter 2's homework for you, you lack the foundation for Chapter 3, and no amount of AI assistance can compensate for missing foundations. By midterm, you're underwater.

The students who use AI well in math and science use it to understand, not to solve. That's what this chapter teaches.

AI for Math: The Right Way

Understanding, Not Answering

The fundamental shift in how to use AI for math:

Wrong approach: > "Solve the integral of x^2 * sin(x) dx"

Right approach: > "I need to integrate x^2 * sin(x) dx. I know I should use integration by parts, but I'm not sure how to pick u and dv when one factor is polynomial and the other is trigonometric. Can you explain the decision-making process for choosing u and dv in these cases? Don't solve this specific problem yet — help me understand the general strategy."

The first gives you an answer. The second gives you a skill.

Step-by-Step Diagnostic

When you get a math problem wrong, AI pinpoints exactly where your reasoning broke down:

```
I'm working on this problem: [state the problem]
Here's my work, step by step:
Step 1: [your work]
Step 2: [your work]
Step 3: [your work]
...
I got [your answer] but the answer should be [correct answer].

Find the exact step where I went wrong and explain:
1. What error I made (computational? conceptual? notational?)
2. Why that error happened (what was I probably thinking?)
3. How to avoid this type of error in the future
4. The correct reasoning for that step

Then let me redo the problem from the error point forward.
```

This beats seeing a correct solution, because you learn from your specific mistake rather than memorizing someone else's approach.

Building Intuition

Math gets much easier once you understand why techniques work, not just how to execute them:

```
I can follow the steps of [technique, e.g., "Gaussian elimination" or
"the chain rule" or "proof by induction"], but I don't understand WHY
it works. Can you explain the underlying intuition?

Don't just give me the formal justification – help me develop a mental
model for why this technique produces correct results. Use a concrete
example to illustrate.
```

Practice Problem Generation

```
I'm studying [topic, e.g., "double integrals" or "eigenvalues" or
"Taylor series"]. Generate 5 practice problems at increasing difficulty:
1. Straightforward application of the technique
2. Requires choosing the right technique from options
3. Requires combining this technique with another we've learned
```

```
4. Includes a common trap or edge case
5. Exam-level difficulty that tests deep understanding

Give me just the problems first. I'll work through them, then show
you my solutions.
```

The "Why Does This Work?" Approach

```
In my [math course], we use the following theorem/formula/technique:
[state it]

I can use it, but I don't understand it deeply. Answer these questions:
1. What problem does this solve? Why was it invented?
2. What's the intuitive idea behind it (before the formal math)?
3. What would go wrong if we didn't have this – what mistakes would
   we make?
4. Can you give me an example where applying it incorrectly gives
   an obviously wrong answer, so I can see what it's protecting against?
```

AI for Physics

Physics combines mathematical reasoning with physical intuition, and AI helps develop both.

Conceptual Understanding

```
I'm learning about [physics concept, e.g., "electromagnetic induction"
or "wave-particle duality" or "Lagrangian mechanics"]. I can plug
numbers into the equations, but I don't have a physical intuition for
what's happening.

Help me build that intuition:
1. Describe a physical scenario where this concept is clearly visible
2. Walk me through what's happening physically (forces, energies,
   fields – whatever is relevant) before introducing any math
3. Show me how the equations capture what I just described physically
4. Give me a scenario where my intuition might lead me astray and
   explain why the math gives a different answer than I'd expect
```

Problem-Solving Strategy

Physics problems often stump students not because the math is hard but because they don't know how to set up the problem. AI helps with the setup without doing the solution:

```
Here's a physics problem: [state the problem]

I'm not sure how to approach it. Without solving it, help me:
1. Identify what type of problem this is (energy conservation?
   Newton's laws? Circuit analysis?)
2. What physical principles apply?
3. What should my free body diagram / circuit diagram / system
   diagram look like?
4. What are the key variables and which ones do I know vs. need
   to find?
5. What equations connect the known and unknown variables?

Let me do the actual solving once I have the setup right.
```

Dimensional Analysis Check

```
I got [answer with units] for this problem: [problem description].
Does this answer make physical sense? Check:
1. Are the units correct?
2. Is the magnitude reasonable? (Is this a physically plausible number?)
3. Does it behave correctly in limiting cases? (What happens if
   mass goes to zero, or velocity is very large, etc.?)
```

This is a real physics skill — checking whether your answer makes physical sense — and AI helps you practice it.

AI for Chemistry

Reaction Understanding

```
I'm studying [reaction type / organic mechanism / equilibrium concept].
I can balance the equation, but I don't understand why this reaction
happens. Explain:
1. What drives this reaction? (Thermodynamics? Kinetics? Both?)
2. What's happening at the molecular/atomic level?
3. How would I predict that this reaction would occur if I hadn't
   been told?
4. What similar reactions follow the same pattern?
```

Lab Report Analysis

```
I ran an experiment on [procedure]. Here are my results:
[your data]
```

```
The expected results were [expected values]. My results [match / don't
match] the expected values.

Help me analyze this WITHOUT writing my lab report for me:
1. Are my results within reasonable experimental error?
2. If my results are off, what sources of error are most likely?
3. What statistical analysis should I perform on this data?
4. What conclusions can I legitimately draw from these results?
5. What can't I conclude from this data? (Overinterpretation is a
   common lab report mistake)
```

Organic Chemistry Mechanisms

Organic chemistry is notoriously difficult because it requires visualizing molecular-level processes. AI helps:

```
Walk me through the mechanism of [reaction] step by step. For each step:
1. What's the nucleophile and what's the electrophile?
2. Why does this particular bond break/form?
3. What's the intermediate?
4. Draw the electron-pushing arrows (in text description)

Then give me a similar reaction and let me try to predict the mechanism
before you confirm or correct.
```

AI for Biology

Systems Understanding

Biology often demands understanding complex systems with many interacting components:

```
I'm studying [system, e.g., "the immune response" or "gene regulation"
or "ecosystem dynamics"]. I understand the individual components but
not how they work together. Can you:
1. Walk me through the process from start to finish
2. At each step, explain WHY that step happens (what triggers it?)
3. Explain what happens if one component fails
4. Give me a "trace" – a specific example following a specific
   [molecule / organism / signal] through the entire process
```

Data Analysis in Biology

```
I have this dataset from my [biology/ecology/genetics] course:
[describe your data]

Help me think through the analysis:
1. What type of statistical test is appropriate for this data?
2. What assumptions does that test make, and does my data meet them?
3. What would a statistically significant result mean in biological
   terms? What would a non-significant result mean?
4. What are the limitations of conclusions I can draw from this
   sample size / experimental design?

Don't run the analysis for me – help me understand which analysis
to run and why.
```

AI for Computer Science (Theory)

For coding-specific guidance, see Chapter 10. Here we'll focus on CS theory:

Algorithm Understanding

```
I'm studying [algorithm, e.g., "Dijkstra's algorithm" or "merge sort"
or "dynamic programming"]. I can memorize the steps, but I want to
understand the insight behind it:
1. What problem does this algorithm solve?
2. What's the naive/brute force approach, and why is it too slow?
3. What key insight makes this algorithm better?
4. Walk me through a small example, showing why the algorithm makes
   each decision it makes
5. What are the limitations? When does this algorithm perform poorly?
```

Complexity Analysis

```
I need to analyze the time complexity of this algorithm/code:
[describe or paste code]

Don't just tell me the Big-O – walk me through the analysis:
1. What operations happen and how many times?
2. How do I count the total operations as a function of input size?
3. What's the worst case? Average case? Best case?
4. How do I handle nested loops, recursion, or conditional branches
   in the analysis?
```

Working with Data

Data analysis shows up across disciplines — in lab courses, social science research, and increasingly in the humanities.

Understanding Statistical Concepts

```
My professor says we need to run a [statistical test] on our data.
I know the formula, but I don't understand:
1. What question does this test actually answer?
2. What are the assumptions, and what happens if they're violated?
3. How do I interpret the output (p-value, test statistic, confidence
   interval)?
4. What's the difference between statistical significance and
   practical significance in this context?

Explain this without assuming I'm a statistics major.
```

Data Visualization Decisions

```
I have data showing [describe your data – variables, types, sample size].
I need to create a visualization for my [paper / lab report / presentation].
Which type of chart or graph best represents this data, and why? What
common mistakes should I avoid in presenting this type of data?
```

The Verification Imperative

Math and science are where AI errors can be most confidently checked — and most dangerous if missed.

Always verify AI's math. AI models make arithmetic errors, apply formulas incorrectly, or pick the wrong technique. If AI solves a problem for you and you submit the answer without checking, you own any errors. More importantly, if AI's answer is wrong and you can't tell, that's evidence you don't understand the material well enough.

Check units and dimensions. If AI gives you a velocity in kilograms, something went wrong. Dimensional analysis is a powerful error-detection tool.

Test against known results. If AI's approach should reduce to a known result in a special case (like classical mechanics being the low-speed limit of relativity), check that it does.

Compare with your textbook. Your textbook is the authoritative source for your course. If AI gives you a formula or definition that differs from your textbook, the textbook wins.

Building Independence

The goal of using AI in math and science courses is to eventually not need it for the types of problems you've practiced. Here's how to build toward independence:

1. **Use AI to learn the approach** for a new type of problem
2. **Practice with AI assistance** — having it check each step
3. **Practice without AI** — working problems on your own, then checking with AI afterward
4. **Test under exam conditions** — no AI, no notes, timed

Skip steps 3 and 4 and you'll feel confident going into the exam, then discover painfully that you can't perform without the safety net.

The best math and science students don't just know how to solve problems — they understand why the solutions work, recognize when their answers don't make sense, and tackle novel problems that don't match any template they've seen. AI is a tool for building those capabilities. It's not a replacement for them.

Chapter 9: Humanities and Social Sciences

Where AI Helps Most and Hurts Most

Humanities and social sciences present a paradox for AI use. On one hand, these are the disciplines most concerned about AI-generated writing, most likely to have restrictive policies, and most focused on the kind of original, interpretive thinking AI struggles to replicate. On the other, AI can be extraordinarily useful for the research, analysis, and argumentative development these disciplines demand.

The key insight: in STEM, AI's value is often in computation — doing calculations faster and more accurately. In the humanities and social sciences, AI's value is in conversation — a thinking partner who helps you develop, challenge, and refine your ideas. The outputs differ, but the principle is the same: AI should make your thinking better, not replace it.

Literary Analysis

Developing Your Reading

The first challenge in literature courses isn't writing about texts — it's reading them deeply enough to have something interesting to say. AI helps you read more carefully, not more carelessly.

Before reading a text:

```
I'm about to read [text] for my [course]. Without spoiling the plot or
giving me interpretations, can you:
1. Tell me the historical and cultural context in which this was written
2. Mention any literary techniques or forms I should watch for
3. Suggest 2-3 questions to keep in mind while reading that will help
   me read more actively
4. Note any aspects of the language that might be challenging (archaic
   language, dialect, translation issues)
```

This primes your reading. You notice things you would have missed, and you read actively instead of passively.

After reading a text:

```
I just finished reading [text]. Here are my initial reactions and thoughts:
[your unfiltered reactions – what struck you, what confused you, what
you noticed]

Help me develop these into more sophisticated analytical observations:
1. Which of my reactions are most intellectually productive to pursue?
2. Are any of my observations connected to larger themes or patterns?
3. What textual evidence should I look at more closely to support
   these observations?
4. What critical lens (feminist, postcolonial, Marxist, psychoanalytic,
   ecocritical, etc.) would best illuminate what I noticed?
```

Notice that you start with YOUR reactions. AI isn't telling you what to think about the text — it's helping you think more rigorously about what you already noticed.

Building Arguments About Literature

```
I'm writing about [text] and I want to argue that [your thesis].
Before I start writing, challenge this argument:
1. Is this thesis specific enough to be interesting, or is it something
   anyone who read the text would agree with?
2. What textual evidence supports it most strongly?
3. What textual evidence seems to contradict it?
4. Has this argument been made before? If so, how can I make it fresh?
5. What's the "so what" – why does this interpretation matter?
```

The most common feedback on student literary essays is "this is more summary than analysis" and "this argument is too obvious." AI helps you avoid both by pushing your thesis toward greater specificity and originality.

Working with Secondary Sources

Literature courses increasingly require engagement with literary criticism and theory. AI helps you understand dense critical texts:

```
I'm reading [critic]'s essay "[title]" for my literature class. The
main argument seems to be [your understanding]. I'm having trouble with:
- [specific section or concept that's unclear]
```

```
Can you help me understand this passage without just replacing my need
to read it? Explain the conceptual framework [critic] is using, and
help me see how it applies to [the primary text we're studying].
```

History

Contextual Understanding

History demands understanding not just what happened but why, and how events connect to broader patterns. AI excels at providing context:

```
I'm studying [historical period/event] for my [course]. Help me
understand the context:
1. What were the major political, economic, and social conditions
   that made this event possible?
2. What were the key debates among contemporaries? (Not everyone
   agreed – what were the factions?)
3. How has historical interpretation of this event changed over time?
   (What did historians in the 1950s think vs. historians today?)
4. What are the primary sources that historians rely on for this
   period, and what are their limitations?
```

Historiographical Awareness

Upper-level history courses care less about "what happened" and more about "how do historians argue about what happened." AI helps you navigate historiography:

```
I'm writing about [historical topic]. I need to understand the major
historiographical debates:
1. What are the main schools of thought on this topic?
2. Who are the key historians associated with each interpretation?
3. What evidence does each side emphasize?
4. What's the current scholarly consensus, if there is one?
5. Are there emerging perspectives that challenge the older debates?
```

This positions your own argument within the scholarly conversation — a critical skill in history.

Source Analysis

```
I have this primary source: [describe or quote the source]
Help me analyze it:
```

```
1. Who created it, when, and for what audience?
2. What biases or perspectives does the creator bring?
3. What does this source reveal that the creator didn't intend to reveal?
4. How does this source relate to [the broader topic of my paper]?
5. What CAN'T this source tell us? What are its limitations as evidence?

Don't interpret the source for me - help me ask better questions of it.
```

Philosophy

Understanding Arguments

Philosophy demands precise logical thinking. AI is surprisingly good at helping you dissect arguments:

```
I'm studying [philosopher]'s argument about [topic] from [text].
I've read it, but I'm not sure I follow the logic completely.

Without just summarizing the argument, help me:
1. Identify the premises (what does [philosopher] assume or assert?)
2. Identify the conclusion (what does the argument try to prove?)
3. Show me the logical structure (how do the premises lead to the
   conclusion?)
4. Identify the weakest premise - the one most vulnerable to criticism
5. What's the strongest objection to this argument?
```

Developing Philosophical Arguments

```
I want to argue that [your philosophical position]. Before I write,
help me think through the argument rigorously:
1. What are my key premises?
2. Are any of my premises controversial? (If they are, I need to
   defend them.)
3. Does my conclusion follow logically from my premises?
4. What are the two or three strongest counterarguments?
5. Are there thought experiments that test my position in
   interesting ways?
```

Engaging with the Canon

```
I need to compare [Philosopher A]'s view on [topic] with [Philosopher B]'s.
Help me understand the key differences WITHOUT simply describing both
views. Instead:
1. What's the fundamental disagreement between them?
```

2. What assumptions do they share despite disagreeing?
3. What evidence or argument would settle the debate between them?
4. Which position is more vulnerable to criticism, and why?

Political Science and Government

Policy Analysis

I'm analyzing [policy or political issue] for my [course]. Help me think through the analysis:
1. What are the main arguments for and against this policy?
2. What theoretical framework should I use (realism, liberalism, institutionalism, constructivism)?
3. What empirical evidence is most relevant?
4. What are the key trade-offs?
5. What do different stakeholders want, and why?

I need to write an analytical paper, not an opinion piece – help me maintain academic objectivity while still having a clear argument.

Understanding Political Theory

I'm reading [theorist]'s work on [concept]. Translate the key ideas into concrete examples:
1. When [theorist] says [concept], what does that look like in practice?
2. Give me a current real-world example that illustrates this concept
3. Give me a current real-world example that CONTRADICTS this concept
4. How has this concept been criticized by other theorists?

Psychology

Understanding Research Methods

I'm reading a psychology study that uses [method: experiment, survey, longitudinal study, meta-analysis, etc.]. Help me evaluate it:
1. What are the strengths and limitations of this method for studying [the topic]?
2. What confounding variables might affect the results?
3. Can I generalize these findings to other populations? Why or why not?
4. What would a replication study need to do differently?
5. How does this study's effect size compare to what's typical in this area of research?

Applying Theoretical Frameworks

I need to analyze [behavior/phenomenon/case study] using [theoretical framework: cognitive behavioral, psychodynamic, humanistic, biological, sociocultural, etc.]. Help me think through how each aspect of the framework applies:
1. How does this framework explain the phenomenon?
2. What aspects of the phenomenon does this framework capture well?
3. What does it miss or explain poorly?
4. What would a therapist/researcher from this perspective recommend?
5. How would an alternative framework explain the same phenomenon differently?

Sociology and Anthropology

Social Analysis

I'm writing about [social phenomenon] for my sociology class. Help me develop a sociological analysis:
1. What social structures, institutions, or norms are relevant?
2. How do factors like class, race, gender, and culture intersect in this phenomenon?
3. What sociological theories (functionalism, conflict theory, symbolic interactionism, etc.) best explain what's happening?
4. What empirical evidence would strengthen my analysis?
5. How does this phenomenon look different from different social positions?

Ethnographic Thinking

I'm learning about [culture/community/social group] in my anthropology course. Help me think ethnographically:
1. What etic (outsider) assumptions might I be bringing that I should question?
2. How might the emic (insider) perspective differ from my initial understanding?
3. What questions would be most productive to investigate?
4. What ethical considerations should guide research in this context?
5. How do I avoid essentializing or stereotyping while still making generalizations?

Language Learning

AI is transforming language learning because it solves the biggest bottleneck: practice with a patient, knowledgeable conversation partner.

Conversational Practice

```
Let's have a conversation in [language] about [topic]. Rules:
- Stay at [A1/A2/B1/B2/C1] level
- If I make a grammatical error, note it in [brackets] with the
  correction, then continue the conversation naturally
- If I use an English word because I don't know the [language] word,
  teach me the word and move on
- Periodically use one vocabulary word I probably don't know, and
  if I ask about it, explain it
- Keep the conversation flowing naturally
```

Grammar Practice

```
I'm struggling with [grammar concept, e.g., "the subjunctive in Spanish"
or "adjective declension in German" or "aspect in Russian"]. Give me:
1. A clear explanation of when and why this grammar feature is used
2. 5 example sentences with translations
3. 5 sentences where I need to fill in the correct form
4. 3 sentences where I need to choose between this form and a similar one
   (to test whether I understand the distinction)
```

Writing in a Foreign Language

```
I wrote this paragraph in [language]: [your text]

Please:
1. Correct any grammatical errors (show original vs. corrected)
2. Note any vocabulary choices that are correct but unnatural (what
   would a native speaker say instead?)
3. Rate my text: beginner / intermediate / advanced
4. Suggest one grammatical structure I could add to make it more
   sophisticated
```

The Critical Thinking Question

The humanities and social sciences are, fundamentally, about critical thinking — the ability to analyze, evaluate, and construct arguments. There's a legitimate concern that AI use might undermine this development.

Here's my honest assessment: AI either accelerates or erodes your critical thinking skills, depending entirely on how you use it.

AI accelerates critical thinking when you use it as a sparring partner — challenging your arguments, asking you to defend your positions, pointing out weaknesses in your reasoning, and exposing you to perspectives you hadn't considered. This is essentially what a good seminar does, available on demand.

AI erodes critical thinking when you use it to generate arguments rather than develop your own. If AI tells you what to think about a text, a historical event, or a social phenomenon, you're outsourcing the cognitive work these courses are designed to develop.

The litmus test: are you thinking harder because of AI, or less?

A Note on AI Detection in Humanities

Humanities papers are where AI detection is most aggressively deployed and most problematic. Humanities professors read many papers on similar topics and develop a strong sense of each student's writing voice, argumentative sophistication, and analytical habits. A paper that suddenly reads differently from a student's previous work raises flags no algorithm is needed to trigger.

The best defense against false suspicion is consistency: if your papers throughout the semester show a clear voice and steady development, and your in-class contributions show the same level of understanding, no one questions your integrity. If your submitted work is dramatically better than your in-class performance, questions will arise — fairly or not.

Use AI to develop your thinking. Do the writing yourself. The gap between AI-polished writing and AI-generated writing is visible to experienced readers, and your authentic voice — developed over the semester — is your best protection.

The Bottom Line

The humanities and social sciences ask you to do the hardest thing AI can help with and the hardest thing AI can't do for you: think deeply about complex, ambiguous, human questions. AI provides context, challenges your arguments, explains difficult texts, and helps you organize your ideas. It can't have original insights, genuine reactions to art, or the interpretive creativity that makes great humanistic scholarship.

Use AI for what it does well. Do the thinking yourself. The combination beats either one alone.

Chapter 10: STEM Projects and Labs

Code, Circuits, and Calculations

STEM projects and labs differ fundamentally from essays and research papers. The output isn't text to be interpreted — it's code that runs, circuits that function, structures that hold, and data that proves something. AI's role shifts accordingly: less about developing arguments, more about building, debugging, and understanding systems.

This chapter covers coding assignments, engineering projects, scientific analysis, and technical documentation — the hands-on work that defines STEM education.

AI for Coding Assignments

Coding is where AI assistance is both most capable and most controversial in education. GitHub Copilot writes entire functions. ChatGPT generates complete programs from natural language descriptions. Claude debugs complex codebases. The temptation to let AI write your code is enormous.

And yet the students who let AI write their code are the ones who can't code when it matters — in interviews, on timed exams, in professional settings where they need to understand and modify complex systems.

The Right Way to Use AI for Code

For learning new syntax and concepts:

```
I'm learning [language] and I don't understand [concept, e.g.,
"list comprehensions in Python" or "pointers in C" or "async/await
in JavaScript"]. Can you:
1. Explain the concept in plain language
2. Show me a simple example with comments explaining each line
3. Show me a more complex example that demonstrates why this
   concept is useful
4. Give me a small exercise to try myself
```

For debugging:

```
My code is supposed to [expected behavior] but instead it [actual behavior].
Here's the code: [your code]
Here's the error message: [error, if any]

Don't fix it for me. Instead:
1. Explain what the error message means
2. Point me to the area of the code where the problem likely is
3. Explain what concept or technique I'm misunderstanding
4. Give me a hint about how to fix it
5. Let me try to fix it and come back if I'm still stuck
```

For understanding existing code:

```
I need to understand this code for my class: [code]
Walk me through it line by line:
1. What does each line do?
2. How does data flow through the program?
3. What design patterns or techniques is this code using?
4. If I needed to modify it to [new requirement], where would I
   make changes?
```

For algorithm implementation:

```
I need to implement [algorithm] in [language]. I understand the
algorithm conceptually – here's my pseudocode:
[your pseudocode]

Before I start coding, tell me:
1. Is my pseudocode correct?
2. What edge cases should I handle?
3. What data structures would be most efficient?
4. Are there any language-specific features that make this
   implementation easier or more idiomatic?

Don't write the code. Let me implement from my corrected pseudocode.
```

What Not to Do

Don't paste the assignment description into AI and submit the output. This is the most common form of coding-related academic dishonesty, and it's increasingly easy to detect. Your professor knows what AI-generated code looks like — more polished, better commented, more uniformly styled than student code. More importantly, if you can't explain your code in office hours or a code review, the game is up.

Don't use Copilot on auto-pilot. Copilot's inline suggestions are seductive — you start typing and it completes the thought. For learning, this short-circuits the process of figuring out what to write. Turn off automatic suggestions and invoke Copilot manually only when you're stuck on a specific piece.

Don't skip the "understand" step. If AI helps you solve a problem, make sure you can solve a similar problem without it. Write the solution again from memory. Explain it to a study partner. Implement it in a different language. If you can't do any of these, you didn't learn — you transcribed.

The Code Review Approach

One of the most valuable ways to use AI for coding assignments:

```
I've written this code to solve [problem]: [your code]
Please review it as if you're a senior developer doing a code review:
1. Does it correctly solve the problem?
2. Are there any bugs or edge cases I'm missing?
3. How could the code be more efficient?
4. How could the code be more readable?
5. Does it follow best practices for [language]?
6. What would you comment on if this were a pull request?
```

This teaches you to think about code quality, not just correctness — a skill that distinguishes you professionally.

Engineering Projects

Engineering coursework often involves design problems — open-ended challenges where you make decisions, justify trade-offs, and produce a working solution.

Design Decision Support

```
I'm designing [system/structure/circuit/mechanism] for my [engineering
course] project. The requirements are: [list requirements]

I'm considering these approaches:
Approach A: [description]
Approach B: [description]

Help me think through the trade-offs:
1. What are the strengths and weaknesses of each approach?
```

```
2. What constraints or requirements favor one over the other?
3. What failure modes should I consider for each?
4. What would an experienced engineer consider that I might be missing?
5. What questions should I be asking that I haven't asked?
```

Calculations Check

```
I'm doing calculations for my [engineering project]. I calculated
that [parameter] = [your value] using [your method].

Check my work:
1. Is my approach correct for this type of problem?
2. Does my answer seem physically reasonable? (magnitude, units,
   sign)
3. What assumptions am I making, and are they valid?
4. What safety factors should I apply?
```

Technical Report Writing

Engineering reports follow specific conventions that AI can help you meet:

```
I need to write the [section: introduction / methodology / results /
discussion] of my engineering report about [project]. Here are my
notes: [your raw notes]

Help me organize these into a professional engineering report section.
Don't write it for me, but:
1. What information should this section include?
2. What's the expected structure for this type of report?
3. What level of technical detail is appropriate?
4. What tables, figures, or diagrams should I include?
5. What are common mistakes students make in this section?
```

Lab Work

Pre-Lab Preparation

```
I have a lab tomorrow on [topic/procedure]. The lab manual says
we'll be doing [brief description]. Help me prepare:
1. What's the underlying theory I should understand before the lab?
2. What are the critical steps where mistakes are most common?
3. What should I expect to observe if the experiment works correctly?
4. What safety considerations are relevant?
5. What data should I be recording, and what format should I use?
```

Data Analysis

```
I collected the following data in my lab: [your data]

The experiment was designed to [purpose]. Help me analyze this
data appropriately:
1. What type of graph should I create for this data?
2. Should I calculate a trendline? What type?
3. How do I calculate the error/uncertainty in my measurements?
4. What statistical analysis is appropriate?
5. Does my data support or contradict the expected result, and
   how confidently?

Walk me through the analysis process. I'll do the calculations
myself, but I need to know what calculations to do.
```

Understanding Discrepancies

```
In my lab, the theoretical value for [measurement] is [value], but
I measured [your value]. That's a [%] difference.

Help me think through why:
1. Is this level of discrepancy normal for this type of measurement?
2. What systematic errors could explain the difference?
3. What random errors could contribute?
4. Could my calculation be wrong? (Here's my calculation: [your work])
5. What would I do differently next time to reduce error?

Important: I need to understand this for my lab report, not just get
a list of error sources. Help me reason through which errors are most
likely given my specific setup and results.
```

Lab Report Best Practices

The lab report is a distinct genre of scientific writing with its own conventions:

```
Review my lab report for [experiment]:
[your report]

Evaluate it against standard lab report expectations:
1. Abstract: Does it summarize purpose, method, key results, and
   conclusion concisely?
2. Introduction: Does it provide enough theory without being a
   textbook chapter?
3. Methods: Could someone replicate my experiment from this description?
```

```
4. Results: Are my graphs and tables properly labeled and formatted?
   Am I presenting data without interpreting it in this section?
5. Discussion: Am I analyzing my results, not just restating them?
   Do I address sources of error thoughtfully?
6. Conclusion: Does it answer the original question?
```

Technical Documentation

Whether you're documenting code, engineering designs, or experimental procedures, technical writing is a distinct skill:

```
I need to write documentation for [code/system/design]. Help me think
about what needs to be documented:
1. Who is the audience? (Other students? Future me? A professional?)
2. What does someone need to know to use/understand/modify this?
3. What assumptions am I making that I should state explicitly?
4. Where should I include examples?
5. What are the common pitfalls someone should be warned about?
```

Team Projects in STEM

Many STEM courses include team projects — designing a system, building a prototype, conducting a group experiment. AI helps with coordination:

Project Planning

```
Our team of [number] needs to complete [project description] by [date].
The deliverables are: [list]

Help us create a project plan:
1. What are the major work packages?
2. Which tasks can be done in parallel?
3. What are the dependencies (what has to be done before what)?
4. How should we divide work given [number] team members?
5. What milestones should we set to stay on track?
```

Integration

```
Our team built different components of [project]:
- Person A built [component]
- Person B built [component]
- Person C built [component]

We need to integrate them. Help us think through:
```

```
1. What interfaces need to match between components?
2. What integration tests should we run?
3. What are the most likely integration problems?
4. What's the best order to integrate in?
```

The Academic Integrity of STEM AI Use

STEM courses have some unique integrity considerations:

Code originality. Most CS courses have honor codes requiring you to write your own code. Using AI to generate code you submit violates this, just as copying from Stack Overflow or another student would. AI being a more sophisticated source doesn't change the principle.

Lab data. Your experimental data must be your own. Never use AI to generate or modify experimental data. This isn't just academic dishonesty — in science, fabricating data is one of the most serious ethical violations possible.

Understanding vs. producing. The STEM standard is usually: can you demonstrate understanding? If AI helped you build something, can you explain every decision, every line of code, every calculation? If yes, you learned. If no, you didn't.

Professor-specific policies. Some CS professors allow Copilot; others prohibit it. Some engineering professors encourage AI for calculations; others want you to do everything by hand. Some lab courses allow AI for data analysis; others don't. Read the syllabus. Ask if unclear.

Building Real STEM Skills

Professors assign coding projects, engineering designs, and lab experiments not to produce artifacts but to develop competencies. The skills you need as a professional STEM worker include:

- Debugging when nothing works and you don't know why
- Making design decisions under uncertainty
- Communicating technical concepts to non-technical audiences
- Working within constraints (time, budget, materials)
- Learning new tools and technologies independently

AI can help you develop all of these skills, but only if you do the work while AI provides support. The student who writes their own code and asks AI for feedback develops debugging skills. The student who asks AI to write the code develops nothing.

Your future employer will expect you to solve problems AI can't — novel problems, ambiguous problems, problems requiring domain expertise and creative insight. The projects and labs you're doing now are practice for that. Don't waste the practice by outsourcing it to AI.

Practical Tips for STEM AI Use

1. **Always attempt the problem yourself first.** Even a failed attempt gives you context that makes AI's help more useful and more educational.
2. **When AI helps you, repeat the work without AI.** Can you do it again independently? If not, you're not done learning.
3. **Ask AI "why" more than "how."** Understanding why a technique works lets you adapt it to new situations. Knowing how to execute it only helps when the next problem looks exactly like this one.
4. **Keep a learning log.** Note what AI helped you understand. Review it before exams. This turns AI conversations into durable study material.
5. **Use AI to go beyond the assignment.** Once you've finished a coding project, ask: "How would a professional improve this?" or "What would break if the input were much larger?" This extra step builds professional-grade thinking.

The best STEM students in 2026 use AI to learn more deeply, not more shallowly. Be one of them.

Part IV: Collaboration and Communication

"If you want to go fast, go alone. If you want to go far, go together."

— African proverb

Chapter 11: Group Projects and Collaboration

The Group Project Problem

Nobody's favorite assignment. Students universally dread group projects, and for good reason: they layer all the complexity of teamwork — coordination, communication, unequal effort, conflicting schedules, different standards — on top of the academic work itself. Professors universally assign them because collaboration is a real professional skill, and the messiness is part of the lesson.

AI can't fix group dynamics. But it can reduce the friction that makes good teams struggle, and give functional teams superpowers. This chapter is about using AI to make group projects less painful and more productive.

AI for Project Planning

The first thing that goes wrong in group projects is the plan — or rather, the absence of one. Most student teams divide work vaguely ("you do the intro, I'll do the analysis") and hope it comes together at the end. It rarely does.

Creating a Project Plan

```
Our team has [number] members and we need to complete [project description]
by [date]. The deliverables are: [list deliverables]

Our professor's grading criteria are: [rubric points if available]

Help us create a project plan:
1. Break the project into specific, well-defined tasks
2. Estimate how long each task will take
3. Identify dependencies (what needs to be done before what?)
4. Suggest a logical division of labor for [number] people
5. Set milestones with dates – when should each major component be done?
6. Build in time for integration and revision before the deadline
```

Share the plan with your team. Adjust it. Any plan beats no plan, and AI can produce a reasonable starting point in a minute.

Role Assignment

```
Our group project on [topic] requires these skills:
- [Research / data analysis / writing / coding / design / presentation]

Team members and their strengths:
- [Name]: [strengths and preferences]
- [Name]: [strengths and preferences]
- [Name]: [strengths and preferences]

Suggest how to assign roles that:
1. Play to each person's strengths
2. Ensure no one is overloaded
3. Build in accountability (each person has clear, measurable deliverables)
4. Allow for skill development (not just doing what you already know)
```

AI for Shared Research

When multiple team members are researching different aspects of the same topic, coordination prevents duplication and ensures coverage.

Research Coordination

Have one team member create a shared research brief:

```
Our group is researching [topic]. We're dividing it as follows:
- Person A is covering [subtopic]
- Person B is covering [subtopic]
- Person C is covering [subtopic]

For each subtopic, suggest:
1. Key search terms and databases
2. Essential background sources everyone should be familiar with
3. Potential overlaps between subtopics that we need to coordinate on
4. Gaps – aspects of [topic] that fall between our subtopics and
   might get missed
```

Synthesizing Team Research

When team members bring their individual research together, AI can help identify connections and conflicts:

```
Here are summaries of what each team member found in their research:
```

```
Person A found: [summary of findings on subtopic A]
Person B found: [summary of findings on subtopic B]
Person C found: [summary of findings on subtopic C]

Help us synthesize:
1. What themes emerge across all three areas?
2. Where do findings contradict each other?
3. What's the most interesting connection between different subtopics?
4. How does this synthesis inform our overall argument/thesis?
5. What gaps remain that we need to address?
```

AI for Team Writing

Writing as a team is notoriously hard. Different members bring different writing styles, quality standards, and interpretations of the assignment. AI can help pull them into consistency.

Style Harmonization

When different team members write different sections, the result often reads like a patchwork. Once everyone has written their sections:

```
Here are sections written by different team members for our [project]:
[Section 1 by Person A]
[Section 2 by Person B]
[Section 3 by Person C]

Identify:
1. Style inconsistencies (tone, formality, level of detail)
2. Formatting inconsistencies (headings, citation style, terminology)
3. Content overlaps (where two sections cover the same thing)
4. Content gaps (where sections don't connect smoothly)
5. Terminology conflicts (where different sections use different
   words for the same concept)

Don't rewrite the sections – flag the issues so we can fix them ourselves.
```

Transition Writing

The connective tissue between sections is where group papers usually fall apart:

```
Here's the end of [Section A] and the beginning of [Section B].
These were written by different team members and don't flow well.
```

```
The main point of Section A is: [summary]
The main point of Section B is: [summary]

Suggest 2-3 transition approaches that would connect these sections
logically. Show me what ideas need to be introduced at the end of A
or the beginning of B to make the connection clear.
```

Peer Review Within the Team

Before submitting, have each team member review other members' sections, and use AI to structure the review:

```
I need to give constructive feedback on my teammate's section of our
group paper. Here's their section: [section]

The assignment requirements are: [requirements]

Help me give useful feedback:
1. What are the strengths of this section?
2. What specific improvements would make it stronger?
3. Are there any factual errors or unsupported claims?
4. How well does this section serve the overall paper?
5. Suggest specific changes rather than vague criticism

I want to be helpful, not harsh. Help me frame feedback constructively.
```

AI for Team Coordination

Meeting Agendas

```
Our team is meeting [tomorrow/this week] to discuss [project].
Current status:
- Person A has completed [X] and is working on [Y]
- Person B has completed [X] and is stuck on [Y]
- Person C has not started yet because they're waiting on [dependency]

Create an efficient meeting agenda that:
1. Prioritizes unblocking Person C
2. Helps Person B get unstuck
3. Checks alignment on the overall direction
4. Sets clear action items with deadlines for each person
5. Can be completed in [time limit] minutes
```

Progress Tracking

```
Our project timeline says we should be at [milestone] by now.
Here's where we actually are:
- [Task 1]: [status]
- [Task 2]: [status]
- [Task 3]: [status]

Assess:
1. Are we on track, behind, or ahead?
2. What's the critical path – which delayed tasks will push back
   the final deadline?
3. What can we do to get back on track?
4. Should we adjust the remaining timeline?
5. What do we need to cut or simplify to meet the deadline?
```

Dealing with Group Dynamics

AI can't fix a dysfunctional team, but it can help you think through the interpersonal challenges.

The Free Rider Problem

```
One of our team members isn't contributing. They've missed [X] meetings
and haven't completed [Y]. Our project is due in [Z] days.

Help me think through options:
1. How do we address this directly with the person?
2. How do we redistribute their work if they don't step up?
3. Should we involve the professor? If so, how and when?
4. How do we protect the rest of the team's grades?
5. What documentation should we keep in case this becomes a dispute?

I want to handle this professionally, not passive-aggressively.
```

Disagreements About Direction

```
Our team disagrees about [issue]. Person A thinks we should [approach A]
because [reasons]. Person B thinks we should [approach B] because [reasons].

Help us evaluate both approaches:
1. What are the strengths of each approach?
2. What risks does each approach carry?
3. Is there a compromise that incorporates the best of both?
```

```
4. What does the assignment actually call for? Does that settle it?
5. If we can't agree, what's a fair decision-making process?
```

Quality Disagreements

```
A team member submitted work that I don't think meets the standard
we need. It's not wrong, but it's [too brief / poorly organized /
doesn't address the rubric / etc.].

Help me figure out how to:
1. Communicate this without damaging the relationship
2. Be specific about what needs improvement
3. Offer to help rather than just criticize
4. Determine if my standard is too high or their work is actually
   below expectations
```

AI Tools for Team Productivity

Beyond general-purpose AI, several tools are particularly useful for team projects:

Shared documents with AI (Google Docs + Gemini, Microsoft Word + Copilot): These let multiple team members write in the same document while using AI for drafting, editing, and formatting. The revision history also shows who contributed what.

NotebookLM for shared research: Create a shared NotebookLM notebook where team members upload their research sources. The whole team can then ask questions across all the sources.

Project management tools: Not AI-specific, but Notion, Trello, and Asana help teams track tasks and deadlines. Several now include AI features for generating task lists, summarizing progress, and drafting updates.

Communication tools: Use a group chat (Slack, Discord, Teams) for coordination. AI can help you draft clear messages when you need to communicate complex decisions or feedback.

Presentations as a Team

Group presentations add another coordination layer. Chapter 12 covers presentations in depth, but here are team-specific tips:

Dividing the Presentation

```
Our group presentation on [topic] needs to be [length] minutes with
[number] speakers. Our content covers:
[outline of what we need to present]

Suggest how to divide this into [number] speaking sections that:
1. Give each speaker a coherent, logical segment
2. Balance speaking time roughly equally
3. Build the presentation's argument progressively
4. Include smooth transitions between speakers
5. Play to each speaker's strengths if possible:
   [Speaker A is good at... / Speaker B is good at...]
```

Rehearsal Planning

```
We need to rehearse our group presentation. We have [time] available
for rehearsal and the presentation is in [days].

Create a rehearsal plan:
1. First run-through: focus on content and timing
2. What to evaluate after the first run
3. Second run-through: focus on transitions and flow
4. What to fix between rehearsals
5. Final run: simulate the actual presentation conditions
```

The Academic Integrity of Group AI Use

Group projects raise unique integrity considerations:

Establish team norms early. At the first meeting, discuss how the team will use AI. If one member uses AI extensively and another doesn't, agree on a standard before it becomes a problem.

Disclose team AI use. If your professor requires AI disclosure, disclose it for the whole team. Be honest about which parts were AI-assisted and how.

AI for coordination is generally acceptable. Using AI to plan, organize, and coordinate is rarely problematic. Using AI to produce the actual deliverables is subject to the same rules as individual assignments.

The workload question. If one team member uses AI to complete their share in an hour while another spends ten hours doing theirs manually, is that fair?

There's no universal answer, but the team should discuss expectations about effort and contribution.

Individual accountability. Even in a group project, you should be able to explain and defend any part of the work. If a professor asks you about a section you didn't write, "that was my teammate's part" is technically true but doesn't demonstrate learning.

Making Group Projects Better

Despite the complaints, group projects teach real skills. The messy parts — miscommunication, conflicting approaches, unequal effort — are what you'll face in every professional team you ever join. AI can reduce the friction, but the human skills of collaboration are yours to develop.

Use AI to spend less time on logistics and more on the work that matters. Use it to communicate more clearly, plan more effectively, and produce more polished results. But the collaboration itself — the negotiation, the compromise, the shared accountability — that's the learning, and no tool can do it for you.

Students who learn to collaborate well in school become professionals who lead successful teams at work. It's one of the most valuable skills you'll develop in college, even though it never feels that way at 10 PM the night before the project is due.

Chapter 12: Presentations and Public Speaking

The Skill Nobody Teaches

You will give more presentations in your career than you will write papers. Board meetings, project updates, client pitches, conference talks, training sessions — professional life runs on presentations. And yet most students get almost no instruction on how to present well. You're assigned presentations, graded on them, and left to figure out the rest yourself.

AI won't make you a great speaker. That takes practice. But it can help you build better slides, structure more compelling talks, anticipate tough questions, and rehearse delivery. Paired with actual rehearsal, AI turns a dreaded assignment into a chance to build a career-defining skill.

Building Your Presentation

Starting with Structure, Not Slides

The most common presentation mistake is opening PowerPoint first. Slides are a visual aid — they support your talk. Build slides before you know what you're saying and you end up reading bullet points to an audience that can read them faster than you can speak them.

Start with your message:

```
I need to give a [length]-minute presentation on [topic] for my
[course] class. The audience is [classmates / professor / mixed].

Before I build any slides, help me structure my talk:
1. What's the single most important thing I want the audience to
   take away?
2. What are the 3-4 key points that support that takeaway?
3. What's the most compelling opening? (Not "Hi, my name is..."
   or "Today I'll be talking about...")
4. What order should I present my points in for maximum impact?
```

```
5. How should I close? (Not just "any questions?" – something
   that reinforces the takeaway)
```

The Presentation Arc

Good presentations tell a story, even when the content is technical or academic:

```
My presentation is about [topic]. Help me create a narrative arc:
1. Opening hook: Something that makes the audience care about this
   topic in the first 30 seconds
2. The problem or question: What tension or gap in knowledge does
   my topic address?
3. The journey: Walk through my key points as a logical progression
4. The resolution: What answer, conclusion, or call to action do I
   arrive at?
5. The landing: A memorable final statement or image

This isn't a TED talk – it's a [class presentation / thesis defense /
conference talk] – so keep the tone appropriate, but help me make it
engaging rather than just informational.
```

From Structure to Slides

Once you know what you're saying, build slides that support — not replicate — your words:

```
Here's the structure of my talk:
[your outline with key points for each section]

For each section, suggest:
1. How many slides this section needs
2. What should be ON each slide (key visual, chart, quote, image –
   not paragraphs of text)
3. What I should be SAYING while each slide is displayed
4. Whether a slide is even necessary (sometimes the speaker without
   a slide is more powerful)

Rules: No more than [total number] slides. No slide should have more
than [6-8] words or a single key visual. I am not creating a document
– I'm creating a visual accompaniment.
```

Slide Design Principles

If you're building slides from scratch:

```
Review my slide content for design effectiveness:
[describe or list your slide contents]

Check for:
1. Text density – are any slides too wordy?
2. Readability – will this be legible from the back of a classroom?
3. Visual hierarchy – does each slide have a clear focal point?
4. Consistency – are fonts, colors, and formatting consistent?
5. Data visualization – are my charts and graphs the right type for
   my data? Are they clearly labeled?
6. Slide count – do I have too many or too few for [length] minutes?
   (Rule of thumb: 1-2 minutes per slide)
```

Preparing Your Content

Simplifying Complex Topics

Academic presentations often require explaining complex material to an audience with varying expertise:

```
I need to explain [complex concept] in my presentation. My audience
includes [description of audience and their likely knowledge level].

Help me:
1. Find the right level of explanation – not too basic, not too
   advanced for this audience
2. Create an analogy that makes the concept intuitive
3. Identify what I can skip and what I absolutely must include
4. Suggest a visual (diagram, flowchart, comparison) that would
   make this clearer than words alone
```

Creating Effective Data Presentations

If your presentation involves data or research findings:

```
I need to present these findings in my talk:
[your data/findings]

Help me figure out:
1. Which findings are most important for my audience?
2. What's the best way to visualize each finding?
3. How do I present statistics without losing my audience?
4. What story does the data tell? How do I build a narrative around it?
```

```
5. What caveats or limitations do I need to mention, and how do I
   do that without undermining my presentation?
```

Thesis and Dissertation Defenses

For graduate students facing defenses:

```
I'm preparing for my [thesis/dissertation] defense on [topic].
My committee includes professors specializing in [areas].

Help me prepare:
1. Structure a [length]-minute presentation of my research
2. What should I emphasize vs. what can I summarize briefly?
3. How do I present my methodology so it's clear to committee
   members outside my subfield?
4. What are the most likely questions my committee will ask?
5. How do I handle "I don't know" moments gracefully?
6. What's the balance between confidence in my work and
   acknowledging limitations?
```

Practicing Delivery

AI can't watch you present, but it can help you prepare specific aspects of delivery.

Anticipating Questions

```
I'm presenting on [topic] to [audience]. After my talk, there will
be a Q&A session.

Based on my presentation content:
[summary of your key points and arguments]

Generate the 10 most likely questions I'll be asked, ranging from:
- Clarification questions ("Can you explain what you meant by...?")
- Challenge questions ("How do you account for...?")
- Extension questions ("Have you considered...?")
- Technical questions about methodology or data

For each question, suggest how I should answer concisely and confidently.
```

Handling Tough Questions

```
I'm worried about being asked [specific difficult question] during
my presentation. Help me prepare:
1. Why might someone ask this question?
```

2. What's a direct, honest answer?
3. If I don't know the answer, how do I handle that gracefully?
4. What bridge phrase can I use to get back to my main points?
5. Is there a related point I can pivot to that strengthens my presentation?

Reducing Filler Words

```
I tend to say "um," "uh," "like," and "you know" a lot when presenting.
Give me:
1. Techniques for reducing filler words
2. What to do instead of saying "um" (hint: it involves silence)
3. Practice exercises I can do before my presentation
4. Specific phrases I can substitute when I feel a filler word coming
```

Timing Your Presentation

```
My presentation needs to be exactly [length] minutes. Here's my outline
with what I plan to say for each section:
[outline with speaking notes]

Estimate how long each section will take at a normal speaking pace
(approximately 130 words per minute for presentation speaking).
Am I over or under? What should I cut or expand?
```

Presentation Formats

The Lightning Talk (3–5 minutes)

```
I need to give a [3/5]-minute presentation on [topic]. That's extremely
short. Help me:
1. Identify the ONE key message I can convey in this time
2. Strip everything down to only what supports that message
3. Plan: 30-second hook, [2-4] minutes of content, 30-second close
4. Create no more than [3-5] slides
5. Practice: write out what I'd say in exactly [number] words
```

The Class Presentation (10–20 minutes)

```
I have [length] minutes to present [topic] to my class. Structure:
1. Engaging opening (1-2 minutes)
2. Context/background (2-3 minutes)
3. Main content with 3-4 key points ([X] minutes)
4. Conclusion and takeaway (1-2 minutes)
5. Q&A time (if applicable)
```

```
Help me allocate time and decide what to include vs. what to cut.
```

The Research Presentation (20–30 minutes)

```
I'm presenting my research on [topic] at [venue: class / conference /
seminar]. I have [length] minutes.

Help me structure this for an academic audience:
1. Motivation: Why does this research matter? (2-3 minutes)
2. Background: What existing work does this build on? (3-5 minutes)
3. Methodology: What did I do and why? ([X] minutes)
4. Results: What did I find? ([X] minutes)
5. Discussion: What does it mean? (3-5 minutes)
6. Future work: What comes next? (1-2 minutes)
```

The Poster Presentation

```
I'm presenting a research poster on [topic] at [event]. Help me:
1. Organize my content for the poster format (visual, scannable,
   not text-heavy)
2. Write concise section headers that guide viewers through my research
3. Decide which visuals (graphs, diagrams, images) to include
4. Prepare a 2-minute "elevator pitch" version of my poster for
   visitors who walk by
5. Prepare for the detailed version – questions from interested
   viewers who want to go deep
```

Overcoming Presentation Anxiety

Public speaking anxiety is real and common. AI can help you prepare in ways that ease it:

Thorough Preparation

The best antidote to anxiety is knowing your material cold. Use AI to surface every possible question, practice your transitions, and verify your facts. When you know you're prepared, anxiety diminishes.

Scripting Key Moments

You don't need to script your entire talk — and shouldn't, because it sounds robotic. But scripting your opening and closing ensures you start and end strong, the moments when anxiety runs highest.

```
Help me write a natural-sounding opening for my presentation on [topic].
It should:
1. Not start with "Hello, my name is..." or "Today I'll be talking about..."
2. Hook the audience's attention immediately
3. Establish why this topic matters to them
4. Transition smoothly into my first point
5. Feel conversational, not scripted – something I can memorize and
   deliver naturally
```

Building Confidence Through Practice

```
I want to rehearse my presentation by explaining my key points to you.
After each point, tell me:
1. Was my explanation clear?
2. Did I include unnecessary details?
3. Would a non-expert understand what I said?
4. How could I say this more concisely?
5. What's a stronger way to transition to my next point?
```

Common Presentation Mistakes

Reading slides. Your slides are for the audience. Your speaking notes are for you. Never read what's on screen — the audience can read it themselves, and they're bored the moment you start.

Too much content. A presentation is not a paper read aloud. You can't cover everything. Better to explain three things well than seven things superficially.

No story. Data, facts, and bullet points don't create engagement. A narrative — even a simple one (problem, investigation, solution) — keeps the audience with you.

Ignoring the audience. Watch for confused faces, disengagement, and nods. Adjust in real time. This skill only develops with practice, but awareness of the audience is the first step.

Ending weakly. "That's it, I guess. Any questions?" is the worst ending. Prepare a strong closing — something that summarizes your takeaway and leaves a lasting impression.

Using AI on Presentation Day

Last-Minute Review

```
My presentation is in [one hour / two hours / tomorrow morning].
Here are my key points: [list them]
Quiz me quickly on each one. Ask me to explain each point as if
you're an audience member. Flag anything I can't explain clearly.
```

After the Presentation

```
I just gave my presentation on [topic]. Here's what went well and
what went badly:
- Went well: [what worked]
- Went badly: [what didn't work]
- Questions I struggled with: [list them]

Help me:
1. Identify patterns in what went wrong (is it preparation, delivery,
   content, or nerves?)
2. Create a specific plan for improving next time
3. Develop answers for the questions I struggled with (so I'm ready
   if they come up again)
```

The Long Game

Presentation skills compound. Every presentation, good or bad, teaches you something. AI accelerates this learning by helping you prepare more thoroughly and debrief more effectively. But the actual skill — standing in front of people and communicating ideas clearly and confidently — only develops by doing it.

Volunteer for presentations when you can. Take the speaking role in group projects. Sign up for conference presentations. Join a debate club or Toastmasters. The discomfort is temporary; the skill is permanent.

AI helps you prepare. You deliver. And with each delivery, you get better.

Part V: Advanced and Specialized Use

“The more I learn, the more I realize how much I do not know.”

— Albert Einstein

Chapter 13: Graduate-Level Research

A Different Game

If you're a graduate student, everything in the previous chapters applies — but you operate at a level where the stakes are higher, the expectations are different, and the opportunities to use AI productively are greater. This chapter addresses the specific challenges of graduate work: comprehensive literature reviews, thesis and dissertation writing, original research methodology, academic publishing, and the advisor relationship.

Graduate students are also most likely to have legitimate, institution-approved reasons to use AI extensively. Many research labs and graduate programs actively encourage AI for research tasks. But the standard for what counts as original contribution is also higher, which makes the integrity questions more nuanced.

Literature Reviews at Scale

An undergraduate literature review might cover 15–20 sources. A graduate literature review might cover 100–200, sometimes more. At this scale, AI isn't a convenience — it's a necessity for managing volume.

Systematic Search Strategy

```
I'm conducting a literature review on [topic] for my [thesis/dissertation/
comprehensive exam]. My research question is: [question]

Help me build a systematic search strategy:
1. What databases should I search? (discipline-specific recommendations)
2. What search strings should I use, including Boolean operators and
   subject headings?
3. What inclusion/exclusion criteria should I apply?
4. How should I document my search process for reproducibility?
5. What's a reasonable date range given my topic?
6. Are there adjacent fields I should also search?
```

Processing Large Volumes of Papers

When you have 200 papers to process, triage is essential:

```
I've downloaded [number] papers from my literature search. I need to
identify which ones are most relevant to my research question: [question]

Here are the titles and abstracts of the first batch:
[list titles and abstracts]

For each paper, assess:
1. Relevance to my specific research question (high/medium/low)
2. Key contribution (in one sentence)
3. Methodology used
4. Whether I should read the full text or just note it as background

Flag any papers that seem like must-reads for my literature review.
```

Important: This is triage, not reading. You still need to read the full text of any paper you include in your review. AI helps you sort the pile — it doesn't replace engagement with the literature.

Identifying Themes and Gaps

Once you've read a substantial body of literature:

```
I've reviewed [number] papers on [topic]. Here are my notes on the
major findings and arguments:
[your organized notes - themes, findings, methodologies, debates]

Help me identify:
1. What are the major theoretical frameworks being used?
2. Where do researchers agree?
3. Where are the active debates?
4. What methodological approaches dominate, and what alternatives
   exist?
5. What are the gaps - questions that haven't been adequately addressed?
6. How does my proposed research address one or more of these gaps?
```

The last question is the crucial one: your literature review should build toward your research question by showing why it needs to be asked.

Writing the Literature Review

Graduate-level literature reviews must synthesize, not summarize. AI can help you move from one to the other:

```
I'm drafting my literature review. Here's a section where I summarize
several papers:
[your draft section]

Help me revise this from summary to synthesis:
1. Am I just describing what each paper found, or am I identifying
   patterns across papers?
2. Where can I group papers by theme rather than discussing them
   one at a time?
3. How can I use the literature to build toward my research question?
4. Am I being critical enough? Where should I evaluate quality of
   evidence rather than just reporting findings?
5. Does this section clearly contribute to my argument for why my
   research is needed?
```

Thesis and Dissertation Writing

Structuring the Document

```
I'm writing a [master's thesis / doctoral dissertation] in [field]
on [topic]. My research involves [brief description of study].

Help me think through the structure:
1. What chapters does a [field] [thesis/dissertation] typically include?
2. What goes in each chapter, and approximately how long should each be?
3. Where does my specific research design fit into this structure?
4. What are common structural mistakes in [field] dissertations?
5. What expectations does my committee likely have for the format?
```

The Introduction Chapter

```
I need to write the introduction chapter of my [thesis/dissertation].
My research question is [question].
My methodology is [brief description].
My key findings are [brief description].

Help me structure an introduction that:
1. Establishes the importance of the topic
2. Identifies the gap in existing knowledge
3. States my research question clearly
4. Previews my approach
5. Outlines the structure of the entire document
6. Does all of this without being either too broad or too narrow
```

```
Don't write it – outline it. I need to write it in my own voice.
```

The Methodology Chapter

Methodology chapters require precision. AI can help you check completeness:

```
Here's my methodology chapter draft:
[your draft]

Review it for:
1. Have I justified my research design? (Not just described it – why
   this approach?)
2. Is my sampling/selection strategy clearly described and justified?
3. Have I addressed reliability and validity (or trustworthiness and
   credibility for qualitative research)?
4. Have I described my data collection procedures in enough detail
   for replication?
5. Have I explained my analysis approach clearly?
6. Have I addressed ethical considerations and IRB approval?
7. Have I acknowledged limitations of my methodology?
```

The Discussion Chapter

```
My results show [summary of findings]. Help me think through the
discussion:
1. How do my findings relate to the literature I reviewed?
2. Do my results support, contradict, or extend existing theories?
3. What are the theoretical implications?
4. What are the practical implications?
5. What are the limitations of my study?
6. What directions for future research do my findings suggest?
7. What's the contribution – what does my field now know that it
   didn't know before?
```

Research Methodology

Qualitative Research

```
I'm designing a qualitative study on [topic] using [method: interviews/
focus groups/ethnography/case study/grounded theory/phenomenology].

Help me think through:
1. Is this the right method for my research question? Why or why not?
2. What's an appropriate sample size and sampling strategy?
```

```
3. How should I develop my interview guide / observation protocol?
4. What qualitative analysis approach should I use (thematic analysis,
   constant comparison, narrative analysis, etc.)?
5. How do I establish trustworthiness?
6. What reflexivity considerations should I address?
```

Quantitative Research

```
I'm designing a quantitative study to investigate [research question].
My hypothesis is [hypothesis].

Help me think through:
1. What research design is most appropriate (experimental, quasi-
   experimental, correlational, survey)?
2. What's an appropriate sample size? (help me think through power
   analysis considerations)
3. What are my independent and dependent variables?
4. What potential confounding variables should I control for?
5. What statistical tests will I need?
6. What are the assumptions of those tests, and how do I check them?
```

Mixed Methods

```
I'm considering a mixed methods design for my study on [topic].
Help me evaluate whether this is appropriate:
1. What would quantitative data tell me that qualitative can't?
2. What would qualitative data tell me that quantitative can't?
3. Should I use a sequential, concurrent, or embedded design?
4. How will I integrate the two types of data?
5. What are the practical challenges of mixed methods (time, skills,
   resources)?
```

Data Analysis

Statistical Analysis

```
I have a dataset with [describe your variables, sample size, and
research question]. I plan to use [statistical test].

Before I run the analysis:
1. Is this the appropriate test for my data and question?
2. What assumptions does this test make, and how do I check them?
3. What should I do if assumptions are violated?
4. What effect size measure should I report alongside the test?
```

```
5. How should I handle missing data?
6. What supplementary analyses should I consider?
```

Qualitative Data Analysis

```
I've completed my interviews/observations for my qualitative study.
I have [number] of [interviews/transcripts/field notes] to analyze
using [method].

Help me think through the process:
1. What's my coding strategy (deductive, inductive, or both)?
2. How do I develop my initial code book?
3. How do I move from codes to themes/categories?
4. How do I handle data that doesn't fit my emerging themes?
5. How do I demonstrate rigor in my analysis?
6. What should my codebook look like?
```

Important: AI should not code your qualitative data for you. Immersing yourself in the data and developing interpretive codes is the analytical work that constitutes your scholarly contribution. AI can help you think about your approach, but the interpretation must be yours.

Academic Writing at the Graduate Level

Finding Your Scholarly Voice

```
Here's a paragraph from my thesis/dissertation:
[your paragraph]

Evaluate my writing for graduate-level expectations:
1. Am I hedging too much or too little? (Academic writing requires
   appropriate hedging without undermining confidence)
2. Is my tone appropriately scholarly without being unnecessarily
   complex?
3. Am I positioning myself as a contributor to the scholarly
   conversation or just a reporter of others' work?
4. Are my claims proportional to my evidence?
5. Does this sound like a scholar in training or like a student
   summarizing readings?
```

Writing for Publication

If you're aiming to publish your research:

```
I want to submit my research to [journal/conference]. Here's my draft:
[abstract or full manuscript]

Help me evaluate fit and quality:
1. Does my paper match the scope of this journal/conference?
2. Does my abstract follow the conventions of my field?
3. Is my contribution clearly stated?
4. Do I engage with recent literature that reviewers will expect
   to see cited?
5. What are the most likely reviewer objections?
6. Is the paper the right length for this venue?
```

Working with Your Advisor

AI doesn't replace your advisor. Your advisor provides mentorship, disciplinary expertise, political navigation, and career guidance that AI can't. But AI can help you prepare for advisor meetings and make the relationship more productive.

Preparing for Meetings

```
I have a meeting with my advisor about [topic – chapter draft /
research design / data analysis / career direction].

Help me prepare:
1. What are the specific questions I need answered?
2. What should I bring to the meeting (drafts, data, outlines)?
3. What decisions need to be made?
4. What feedback am I seeking, and what feedback am I NOT ready for?
5. How do I present [problem/challenge] without seeming unprepared?
```

Processing Feedback

```
My advisor gave me this feedback on my [chapter/proposal/manuscript]:
[advisor's feedback]

Help me:
1. Understand what they're actually asking for (sometimes feedback
   is vague)
2. Prioritize: which changes are most important?
3. Develop a revision plan
4. Identify where I disagree with the feedback – and how to raise
   that constructively
```

Managing the Graduate Workload

Graduate students juggle a unique combination of coursework, research, teaching, and writing. AI can help with time management:

```
This semester I need to:
- Complete [coursework requirements]
- Make progress on [thesis/dissertation milestone]
- [Teach / TA for course]
- [Other responsibilities]

My deadline for [major milestone] is [date].

Help me create a realistic weekly schedule that:
1. Protects dedicated blocks of writing/research time
2. Balances TA duties without letting them expand indefinitely
3. Accounts for the reality that some weeks will be more productive
   than others
4. Sets intermediate deadlines for my thesis/dissertation
5. Includes time for professional development (conferences, networking,
   job applications)
```

The Integrity Dimension for Graduate Students

Graduate students face higher integrity standards. Your thesis or dissertation is supposed to be an original scholarly contribution. Here's where the lines fall:

Legitimate uses: AI for literature search, paper triage, understanding complex methods, checking statistical assumptions, improving writing clarity, organizing research, preparing for defenses.

Gray area: Using AI to help frame your theoretical contribution, generate research questions, suggest methodology. These are acceptable as brainstorming but problematic if AI's suggestions become your claimed contribution without genuine intellectual development on your part.

Not acceptable: Having AI generate your analysis or interpretation of data. Presenting AI-drafted sections as your own scholarly voice. Using AI to fabricate or embellish results. Having AI write the contribution statement — the very thing your degree certifies you can do.

The acid test for dissertations: Could you defend every claim, every methodological choice, and every interpretive conclusion in your oral defense? If AI made a choice for you and you can't explain why, that's a problem.

Your degree certifies that you can conduct and communicate original research. If AI did the research or the communication, the degree doesn't mean what it's supposed to mean — and that follows you when you enter the academic or professional job market.

The Graduate Student's AI Toolkit

Daily use: Claude or ChatGPT for writing feedback, concept clarification, and thinking partnership. Perplexity for quick research questions.

Research phase: Semantic Scholar and Consensus for literature discovery. NotebookLM for synthesizing across sources. Elicit for structured literature review.

Writing phase: Claude or ChatGPT for structural feedback, argument testing, and editing. Grammarly for mechanical polish.

Analysis phase: AI for checking statistical assumptions and explaining analytical approaches. Your own analysis for the actual work.

Defense prep: AI for generating potential committee questions and practicing responses.

Used ethically, this toolkit can save a graduate student hundreds of hours over the course of a program — time better spent on the intellectual work that actually constitutes your scholarly contribution.

Use AI to handle the scaffolding. Do the scholarship yourself.

Chapter 14: AI for Students with Disabilities

The Great Equalizer — Almost

AI has the potential to be the most significant accessibility technology since screen readers. For students with disabilities, AI tools can transcribe lectures in real time, convert text to speech and back, simplify dense language, organize scattered thoughts, provide alternative explanations of complex material, and adapt to individual learning needs in ways that traditional accommodations never could.

But potential and reality are different things. Many AI tools have accessibility gaps. Institutional AI policies sometimes fail to account for disability accommodations. And the line between "using AI as an assistive tool" and "using AI to complete assignments" gets harder to draw when AI serves a genuine accessibility function.

This chapter is for students with disabilities who want to use AI effectively, and for all students who want to understand how AI intersects with disability access in education.

AI as Assistive Technology

For Students with Visual Impairments

AI can serve as a visual interpreter, describing images, charts, diagrams, and visual content that screen readers can't process:

```
I'm looking at [a chart/diagram/image] from my [course] textbook.
It's described in the alt text as: [alt text if available]

Please describe this image in detail:
1. What information is being conveyed?
2. What are the key data points or relationships shown?
3. How does this visual support the text it accompanies?
4. Are there any trends, patterns, or outliers I should note?
```

For documents without alt text (unfortunately common in academic materials):

```
I've uploaded an image from my coursework that isn't accessible via
screen reader. Please provide:
1. A detailed description of what's shown
2. Any text visible in the image
3. The key information I need from this visual
4. An alternative way to understand the same information without
   the visual
```

AI-powered tools can also convert documents between formats — turning scanned PDFs into accessible text, or visual diagrams into text descriptions.

For Students with Hearing Impairments

AI-powered transcription has improved dramatically. Tools like Otter.ai, Microsoft Teams transcription, and Google's live captioning produce real-time text versions of lectures and discussions. AI takes these beyond basic transcription:

```
Here's a transcript from my lecture on [topic]. The transcription has
errors because of [background noise / technical terms / professor's
accent]. Help me:
1. Identify and correct likely transcription errors based on the
   subject matter
2. Fill in gaps marked as [inaudible]
3. Organize the raw transcript into logical sections with headers
4. Highlight key terms, definitions, and concepts mentioned
```

For pre-recorded course content without captions:

```
I have a lecture recording without captions. After transcribing it
[using another tool], I need help organizing the content into
study notes. Here's the raw transcript:
[transcript]

Please:
1. Clean up transcription errors
2. Organize into topics and subtopics
3. Identify key concepts, definitions, and examples
4. Flag anything that seems unclear and might need clarification
   from the professor
```

For Students with Learning Disabilities

Dyslexia and reading difficulties:

AI can reformat and simplify text without changing the meaning:

```
I have difficulty with [dense text / long paragraphs / complex sentence
structures]. Here's a passage from my [textbook/article]:
[passage]

Please:
1. Break this into shorter paragraphs
2. Simplify sentence structures without dumbing down the content
3. Define any jargon in parentheses after the term
4. Highlight the key takeaway from each paragraph
5. Keep all the original meaning – don't oversimplify, just make it
   more accessible
```

ADHD and executive function challenges:

AI can help with the organizational work that many students with ADHD find most challenging:

```
I need to write a paper on [topic] and I have a lot of scattered
thoughts. Here's everything in my head right now:
[brain dump – don't worry about organization]

Help me:
1. Sort these thoughts into categories
2. Identify which thoughts are actually about the same idea
3. Suggest an order that makes logical sense
4. Turn this chaos into an outline I can work from
5. Break the writing into small, manageable chunks with clear
   stopping points

I work best in short focused bursts, so suggest how to divide this
into 25-minute work sessions.
```

```
I have these assignments due this week:
[list with due dates]

I'm struggling to prioritize and get started. Help me:
1. Put these in order of urgency and importance
2. Break each assignment into the smallest possible first step
3. Estimate how long each assignment will take
```

```
4. Create a daily schedule that accounts for my tendency to
   procrastinate on [types of tasks I avoid]
5. Include specific "start now" actions – not "work on paper" but
   "open document and write one sentence about your thesis"
```

Dyscalculia:

```
I'm working on [math problem] and I struggle with numerical processing.
Please:
1. Walk me through this problem using words, not just symbols
2. Show each step with an explanation of WHAT we're doing and WHY
3. Use concrete examples or analogies for abstract operations
4. Let me practice each step separately before combining them
5. Use color-coding or formatting to distinguish different types
   of numbers/operations (describe using text formatting since I
   may use assistive technology)
```

For Students with Physical Disabilities

Voice-to-text AI has improved significantly, making it possible to work with AI tools entirely through speech. For students who find typing difficult:

- Most AI platforms support voice input through browser-based or system-level speech recognition
- Dictation tools like Dragon NaturallySpeaking integrate with AI interfaces
- Mobile apps for ChatGPT, Claude, and Gemini support voice conversations

```
I use voice input for all my work. When I ask you to help with writing,
please:
1. Format output in a way that's easy to edit via voice commands
2. Use shorter paragraphs (easier to navigate with voice)
3. Number sections so I can say "go to section 3"
4. When asking me questions, ask one at a time and wait for my response
```

For Students with Autism Spectrum Conditions

AI can help with aspects of academic work that involve ambiguous social expectations:

```
My professor's assignment says to "critically engage with the text."
I'm not sure what that means specifically. Can you:
1. Explain what "critically engage" means in academic writing
2. Give me a concrete example of what it looks like vs. what it
```

```
   doesn't look like
3. Break down the steps of critical engagement into a checklist
4. Show me the difference between summary (which isn't critical
   engagement) and analysis (which is)
```

```
I need to participate in class discussion for a grade. I have trouble
with spontaneous verbal contributions. Help me:
1. Pre-generate 3-4 thoughtful comments or questions about tomorrow's
   reading: [reading topic]
2. Make them specific enough to be useful but flexible enough to
   fit the actual discussion
3. Write them as complete sentences I can read if needed
4. Include follow-up points in case someone responds to my comment
```

For Students with Mental Health Conditions

AI can help manage the academic impact of anxiety, depression, and other mental health conditions:

```
I'm feeling overwhelmed by my workload and I'm struggling to function
academically. I don't need therapy – I need help making my work
manageable right now.

Here's everything on my plate: [list everything]

Help me:
1. Identify what absolutely must be done in the next 48 hours
2. Identify what can be deferred or dropped without serious consequences
3. Create the smallest possible version of each task that would still
   be acceptable to submit
4. Give me a realistic plan for today – just today
5. Remind me that imperfect work submitted is better than perfect
   work not submitted
```

AI and Accommodation Policies

Understanding Your Rights

Under the Americans with Disabilities Act (ADA) and Section 504 of the Rehabilitation Act, students with documented disabilities are entitled to reasonable accommodations. If AI tools serve an accommodation function, you may be entitled to use them even when a professor's policy restricts AI for other students.

This isn't straightforward, however:

- Accommodations are typically arranged through your school's disability services office, not unilaterally
- An accommodation must be related to your documented disability
- Using AI as a general-purpose shortcut is not an accommodation
- Professors may need to be informed that you have accommodation approval for AI use (without necessarily knowing the nature of your disability)

Getting AI Approved as an Accommodation

```
I want to request AI tools as an accommodation for my [disability].
Help me prepare for my meeting with disability services:
1. How do I articulate the specific barrier I face without AI?
2. How does AI specifically address that barrier?
3. What's the difference between using AI as an accommodation and
   using AI as a shortcut? (I need to articulate this clearly)
4. What specific AI uses do I want approved?
5. What documentation might I need?
```

Communicating with Professors

When you have approved AI accommodation but a professor's policy restricts AI:

```
My professor has a no-AI policy, but I have disability services
approval to use AI as an accommodation. Help me draft a professional
email that:
1. References my accommodation letter (without over-sharing about
   my disability)
2. Explains specifically how I'll use AI in their course
3. Assures them that I'm using AI to access the learning, not to
   bypass it
4. Asks for a meeting if they have questions
5. Maintains a respectful, collaborative tone
```

AI Accessibility Limitations

AI tools themselves aren't always accessible, and that's worth naming:

Screen reader compatibility varies. ChatGPT's web interface has improved but isn't perfect with screen readers. Claude's interface is generally better. Mobile apps are often more accessible than web interfaces.

Voice input has limitations. Technical jargon, specialized vocabulary, and non-English terms can trip up voice-to-text systems feeding into AI tools.

Complex outputs can be hard to navigate. When AI generates long, formatted responses (tables, code blocks, lists), navigating them with assistive technology can be cumbersome.

Multimodal features may not be accessible. AI features that rely on image generation, visual output, or video don't serve students who can't perceive those formats.

If you hit accessibility barriers with AI tools, document them and report them. AI companies have accessibility teams, and user feedback drives improvements. Your school's disability services office may also be able to identify more accessible alternatives.

Building Your Accessible AI Workflow

The best approach is to build a consistent workflow that accounts for your specific needs:

```
I have [disability/condition] that affects my academic work in these ways:
[specific impacts on your academic performance]

I currently use these accommodations: [list]

Help me design an AI-augmented study and work workflow that:
1. Addresses my specific challenges
2. Works with my existing accommodations
3. Uses AI tools that are accessible for my needs
4. Stays within academic integrity guidelines
5. Is sustainable across a full semester
```

A Note for All Students

Understanding how AI serves as assistive technology makes you a better collaborator, a more inclusive professional, and a more thoughtful advocate. If a classmate uses AI differently than you do because of a disability, that's their right

— just as a student who uses a calculator isn't "cheating" compared to one who does mental math.

Accessibility accommodations aren't advantages. They're leveling mechanisms that let every student demonstrate what they actually know. When AI serves that function, it's doing exactly what good technology should do.

Resources

- **Your school's disability services office** — start here for formal accommodations
- **AHEAD (Association on Higher Education And Disability)** — guidance on AI and disability accommodations
- **WebAIM** — accessibility resources and tool evaluation
- **AI platform accessibility pages** — most major AI companies publish accessibility documentation
- **Your classmates and community** — disability communities on your campus often share practical tips about what works

If you need accommodation and don't know where to start, contact your school's disability services office. They can help you navigate the intersection of AI policy and disability rights, and they're increasingly prepared for exactly this conversation.

You have every right to use the tools that let you learn. Make sure you're set up to do that.

Part VI: Practical Considerations

"By failing to prepare, you are preparing to fail."

— Benjamin Franklin (attributed)

Chapter 15: Managing Your AI Subscriptions

The $20/Month Question

Every major AI platform wants $20 a month from you. ChatGPT Plus, Claude Pro, Gemini Advanced, Perplexity Pro — they all land on the same price. That's $240/year per subscription, and all four together run nearly $1,000 a year.

For a student, that's real money. A semester of textbooks. Two months of groceries. Half a year of Spotify. You need to be strategic about what you pay for, what you use for free, and what you skip.

This chapter is about getting maximum value from AI on a student budget.

What the Free Tiers Actually Get You

Before spending anything, know what you already have:

ChatGPT Free

- Access to GPT-5.4 (with usage limits)
- File uploads and image analysis
- Web browsing capabilities
- Basic code interpreter
- Mobile app access
- **Limitation:** Once you hit usage limits, you drop to a less capable model. Peak hours burn through limits faster.

Claude Free

- Access to Claude's latest models (with usage limits)
- File and document uploads
- Long-context analysis
- **Limitation:** Stricter usage limits than ChatGPT Free. Heavy study sessions can drain your message allowance. No Projects feature.

Gemini Free

- Access to Gemini models (with usage limits)
- Integration with Google services
- Multimodal capabilities (text, images)
- **Limitation:** Weaker model than Gemini Advanced. No Gemini inside Workspace apps.

Copilot Free

- Access to GPT-5.4 through Microsoft
- Web search integration
- **Limitation:** No Office integration. Lower usage limits.

Perplexity Free

- Unlimited basic searches
- A limited number of Pro searches per day
- Source citations on every search
- **Limitation:** Pro searches — which use stronger models and deeper analysis — are capped.

NotebookLM Free

- Generous source limits
- Audio overview generation
- Document analysis
- **Limitation:** Some advanced features locked.

GitHub Copilot (Student)

- Full Copilot Pro access free with verified student status
- Code completion, chat, and debugging
- **How to get it:** Apply through the GitHub Student Developer Pack at education.github.com

Semantic Scholar

- Completely free
- AI-powered paper summaries

- Citation analysis
- No paid tier

When Free Tiers Are Enough

For most students, free tiers are enough if you:

- Use AI for occasional help, not hours of continuous conversation
- Don't need to upload many documents in a single session
- Can tolerate slower responses at peak hours
- Spread usage across multiple free tools (ChatGPT for some tasks, Claude for others, Perplexity for research)

The multi-tool strategy: Instead of paying for one tool, use the free tiers of several. Hit ChatGPT's limit, switch to Claude. Hit Claude's limit, switch to Gemini. The effect is a much larger free allowance.

When to Pay — and for What

Pay for a subscription when:

1. **You're consistently hitting free-tier limits.** If you run out of messages mid-study-session week after week, a subscription spares you the friction of constant tool-switching.

2. **You need a specific paid feature.** Claude's Projects feature (conversations organized by class or research topic), Gemini's Workspace integration, or Perplexity's unlimited Pro searches might justify the cost based on your workflow.

3. **You're in a research-intensive phase.** Graduate students working on dissertations or undergrads writing major research papers may find a month or two of Perplexity Pro or Claude Pro worth it for that stretch. Subscribe, then cancel — no year-long commitment required.

4. **The time savings beat the money.** If you earn $15/hour at a part-time job and a subscription saves you five hours a month, the math is obvious.

My Recommendations by Budget

Budget: $0/month

ChatGPT Free as your primary tool, Claude Free for document analysis and research, Perplexity Free for source finding, NotebookLM for synthesizing course readings. GitHub Copilot Free (student) for coding. Semantic Scholar for academic paper search.

This stack covers nearly every student need. More tool-switching, but the capabilities are there.

Budget: $10/month

Add **Perplexity Pro** ($20/month, though student or annual discounts sometimes bring it down to roughly $10/month). Research is where students waste the most time, and Perplexity Pro's unlimited deeper searches with citations save hours. Everything else stays on free tiers.

Heavy math/science user? Consider **Wolfram Alpha Pro** ($5/month for students) for computational work.

Budget: $20/month

Pick ONE general-purpose subscription based on your primary use:

- **ChatGPT Plus** for the broadest feature set, the largest ecosystem, and reasoning models for complex problems
- **Claude Pro** for heavy research, writing, and document analysis — Claude's longer context and Projects feature are particularly strong for academic work
- **Gemini Advanced** if you live in Google Workspace (Docs, Sheets, Slides) — the integration makes AI seamless in your existing workflow, plus 2TB of storage

Free tiers cover everything else.

Budget: $40/month

Your primary subscription (ChatGPT Plus, Claude Pro, or Gemini Advanced) plus **Perplexity Pro**. Covers general-purpose AI and research thoroughly.

Budget: More Than $40/month

Unless you have very specific needs, you don't need to go past $40/month. Don't fall into the trap of subscribing to everything. Two well-chosen subscriptions plus free tiers cover every academic use case.

Student Discounts and Free Access

Check these before paying full price:

GitHub Student Developer Pack: Free GitHub Copilot Pro, plus other developer tools. Verify your student status at education.github.com.

Microsoft 365 Education: Many schools provide free Microsoft 365, which may include Copilot features. Ask your school's IT department.

Google Workspace for Education: Your school Google account may unlock AI features unavailable on personal accounts.

School-provided AI access: A growing number of universities offer institutional AI access — sometimes a campus-wide license with ChatGPT, Claude, or another platform. Check your school's IT resources page.

Annual billing discounts: Some AI services discount annual billing – check each platform's pricing page for current options.

Referral programs: Some tools offer free months for referring other users. Check current promotions.

Free trial periods: Most paid tools offer a free trial. Use trials strategically – start one during a heavy research period when you'll get the most value.

The Subscribe-Cancel Strategy

You don't have to commit year-round. Many students benefit from a seasonal approach:

Heavy months (midterms, finals, thesis deadlines): Subscribe to your tool of choice.

Light months (breaks, early semester): Cancel and fall back to free tiers.

Most AI subscriptions are month-to-month with no cancellation penalty. Set calendar reminders to cancel before renewal if you're playing this game.

Important: When you cancel, your data and conversation history are typically preserved. Re-subscribe later and you pick up where you left off.

Avoiding Subscription Creep

Subscription creep — quietly accumulating paid services you barely use — is the financial equivalent of the junk drawer. It happens because:

- Signing up is easy; canceling takes effort
- You forget your subscriptions
- You overestimate future usage based on current excitement
- Free trials auto-convert to paid subscriptions

Prevention strategies:

1. **Audit quarterly.** Every three months, list your subscriptions and ask: did I use this enough to justify the cost?

2. **Track usage first.** Before subscribing, run the free tier for a full week and note how often you hit limits. If you rarely hit them, skip the paid version.

3. **Use a separate email for trials.** Easier to track trial-to-paid conversions and cancel before they charge.

4. **Set calendar reminders.** Start a free trial, set a reminder for one day before it expires.

5. **Use virtual card numbers.** Services like Privacy.com generate single-use card numbers, so trials can't auto-convert.

Family and Group Plans

Some AI services offer family or group plans that let multiple users share a subscription at a lower per-person cost:

- **ChatGPT Team** is built for organizations and requires a minimum user count, so it's rarely practical for informal student groups — but if your club, lab, or student organization qualifies, it's worth a look
- **Google One AI Premium** includes family sharing for the storage component

Check with your study group or friends — a legitimate family or group plan can cut costs sharply. Stay inside the terms of service; sharing individual account credentials is typically prohibited and can get your account terminated.

What's NOT Worth Paying For

AI note-taking apps that just wrap ChatGPT. Many charge $10–20/month for AI features that are a thin layer over models you can access directly. If an app's AI feature is its main selling point and it doesn't offer something genuinely novel, you're paying a markup for a nicer interface.

AI essay writers. Beyond the obvious integrity concerns, these are usually prompt-engineered versions of the same free tools, marketed to desperate students at a premium.

AI tutoring platforms at premium prices. Some charge $50–100/month for "AI tutoring" you can replicate with the free tier of ChatGPT or Claude using the prompts in Chapter 4.

Multiple general-purpose AI subscriptions. ChatGPT Plus AND Claude Pro AND Gemini Advanced is overkill. Pick one. Free tiers handle the rest.

The Total Cost of Being a Student in 2026

Let's put AI costs in context:

Expense	Monthly Cost
Textbooks (amortized)	$50–150

Expense	Monthly Cost
Laptop (amortized)	$25–50
Internet	$30–60
Phone	$30–80
Streaming (1–2 services)	$15–30
AI tools (recommended)	$0–20

AI subscriptions cost less than most tech expenses students already shoulder. The question isn't whether you can afford AI — it's whether a specific subscription beats the free alternatives by enough to justify the price.

For most students, the answer: free tiers are fine, maybe one subscription during heavy stretches. Save the rest for coffee during finals week.

Making the Decision

Here's a simple decision framework:

1. **Run free tiers for two weeks.** Track how often you hit limits and how much it disrupts your workflow.
2. **If you rarely hit limits:** Stay on free tiers. Don't pay.
3. **If you hit limits often:** Identify the tool you hit limits on most. Subscribe to that one.
4. **If you need research depth:** Perplexity Pro is the best research-specific investment.
5. **If you need everything:** One general-purpose subscription plus Perplexity Pro. That's the ceiling for most students.
6. **Re-evaluate every semester.** Your needs shift. A heavy research semester might warrant Pro tools; an elective-heavy semester won't.

The best subscription is the one you actually use enough to justify the cost. Everything else is money you could spend on something that matters more.

Chapter 16: AI and Your Digital Privacy

What You're Giving Away

Every time you type a message into an AI chatbot, you're sending that text to a company's servers. The AI processes your input, generates a response, and — depending on the platform — may store the conversation, use it to train future models, or share aggregated data with partners.

For casual use, this isn't a big deal. But students routinely share things with AI they would never post publicly: personal essays, medical information for a health sciences assignment, financial data for an economics project, original research ideas, proprietary code, deeply personal reflections. Before you share anything with AI, understand what happens to it.

This chapter isn't about making you paranoid. It's about making you informed.

How AI Companies Handle Your Data

The General Model

When you use an AI chatbot, here's the typical flow:

1. **Your input is transmitted** over an encrypted connection to the company's servers
2. **The AI processes your input** and generates a response
3. **The conversation is stored** in your account history so you can return to it
4. **The company may use your conversations** for model improvement — this is where privacy concerns start

Platform-Specific Policies (as of Early 2026)

OpenAI (ChatGPT): - Free tier: Conversations may be used for training unless you opt out in Settings > Data Controls - ChatGPT Plus: Same default, same opt-out - ChatGPT Team/Enterprise: Conversations are not used for training by default - You can delete conversations, but deletion doesn't necessarily pull them from training datasets that already processed them

Anthropic (Claude): - Free and Pro tiers: Conversations may be used to improve models, though Anthropic has committed not to train on data from users who opt out - Claude for Work: Tighter data handling

Google (Gemini): - Conversations may be used to improve Google services - Using Gemini with your school Google account may bring additional protections through the school's data agreement with Google - Data falls under Google's overall privacy policy, which covers every Google service

Microsoft (Copilot): - Consumer Copilot: Data may be used for service improvement - Copilot inside Microsoft 365 Education: Governed by your school's data processing agreement with Microsoft - Enterprise and education data handling is generally more protective

Perplexity: - Search queries and conversations may be used to improve the service - The source of queries (what you searched for) may surface in analytics

How to Opt Out of Training Data Use

On every platform, look for: - **Settings > Privacy** or **Settings > Data Controls** - Options labeled "Improve the model" or "Use my conversations for training" - Toggle these OFF if you don't want your data used for training

Important caveat: Opting out of training use doesn't mean your conversations aren't stored — it means they won't feed future model training. The company still processes and may retain your conversations for service delivery, safety review, and legal compliance.

What You Should Never Share with AI

Regardless of platform or privacy settings, some categories of information should never go into an AI chatbot:

Personal Identification Information

- Social Security numbers
- Financial account numbers
- Passwords or security answers
- Government ID numbers
- Your full name combined with date of birth and address

You'd think this was obvious, but students sometimes paste scholarship applications, financial aid forms, or personal statements containing this information without thinking.

Other People's Private Information

- Classmates' personal information
- Details from confidential conversations
- Student records you have access to as a TA
- Patient information if you're in a healthcare program
- Client information if you're in a legal clinic

FERPA, HIPAA, and professional ethics don't stop applying because you're using AI. A teaching assistant who pastes student grades into ChatGPT to "help with grading" has committed a FERPA violation. A nursing student who discusses a patient case with AI using identifiable information has committed a HIPAA violation.

Proprietary or Confidential Research

If you're working on research that: - Is under a confidentiality agreement - Involves unpublished data - Is part of a funded project with data handling requirements - Includes proprietary information from an industry partner

Don't share that data with AI tools without explicit permission from your PI (principal investigator) or supervisor. Some grants and contracts specifically prohibit sharing data with third-party AI services.

Original Ideas You Want to Protect

Subtler but important: sharing an original research idea, invention, or creative work with AI means sharing it with the company that runs the AI. These companies aren't in the business of stealing student ideas, but the information sits on their servers, runs through their systems, and is potentially accessible to their employees.

For truly original work you might publish, patent, or commercialize, consider: - Using tools with the strongest privacy protections - Opting out of training data use before sharing - Sharing partial information — enough to get help without revealing the whole idea - Asking your institution about AI tools with institutional data agreements

School-Specific Privacy Concerns

School-Provided AI Tools

Many universities now provide AI access through institutional agreements. These typically include:

- **Data stays within the institution's tenant** — not shared with the AI company for training
- **Conversations are governed by the school's data policies** — not the AI company's consumer terms
- **IT administrators may have access** to usage data — know what your school can see

If your school provides an institutional AI tool, use it for sensitive academic work instead of the consumer version. The privacy protections are almost always better.

Learning Management Systems

Some LMS platforms (Canvas, Blackboard, Moodle) are integrating AI features. When you use AI inside your LMS: - Your interactions may be visible to your instructor - Usage data may be tracked and reported - The AI may have access to your course materials, grades, and submissions

Check your school's policies on LMS data collection. You have a right to know what's tracked.

Proctoring Software

AI-powered proctoring tools (Respondus LockDown Browser, Honorlock, ProctorU) record your screen, webcam, and sometimes audio during exams. The privacy concerns are real:

- Video recordings of you in your personal space
- Screen recordings that may capture notifications, browser tabs, or personal content
- Biometric data collection (facial recognition, eye tracking)

- Recordings stored by third-party companies

If proctoring software concerns you: - Ask your school what data is collected and how it's stored - You may be able to request alternative testing arrangements - Students at some schools have successfully challenged mandatory proctoring on privacy grounds - Document any issues you encounter — privacy violations should be reported

Practical Privacy Protection

The Anonymization Approach

When you need AI help on work involving real data or personal situations, anonymize first:

```
Before I share details about my case study / research subject /
personal situation, I'm going to change identifying details.
The core question is the same; only names, locations, and specific
identifiers have been changed. Please help me with:
[your anonymized question]
```

The Segmentation Approach

Don't pour everything into one conversation. On a project with sensitive components, share only what each question needs:

- In one conversation, discuss methodology (without data)
- In another, discuss statistical approaches (with anonymized data)
- In a third, discuss writing (with results but not raw data)

No single conversation holds the complete picture.

Account Hygiene

- **Use separate accounts** for personal and academic AI work when possible
- **Review and delete conversations** you no longer need — especially ones with sensitive information
- **Log out of AI tools** on shared or public computers
- **Don't auto-save passwords** for AI tools on devices you don't fully control

- **Enable two-factor authentication** on every AI account

VPN and Network Considerations

When using AI on public Wi-Fi (library, coffee shop, campus common areas): - Your conversations are encrypted in transit, which protects them from casual snooping - Network administrators can still see that you're connecting to AI services - If privacy from network monitoring matters, use a VPN

The "Free" Product Problem

You've heard the saying: "If the product is free, you are the product." It applies to AI:

Free tiers exist because: 1. They drive adoption and conversion to paid tiers 2. They supply data for model improvement 3. They create ecosystem lock-in

This doesn't mean free tiers are a bad deal — they deliver genuine value. But understand the exchange: you're trading data for a service. Make an informed choice about what data you're comfortable handing over.

Privacy Rights and Regulations

Depending on where you are, you may have specific privacy rights:

In the US: - FERPA protects student educational records - State laws vary — California (CCPA/CPRA), Virginia, Colorado, and others grant rights to access, delete, and opt out of data use - No comprehensive federal privacy law covers AI specifically (as of early 2026)

In the EU: - GDPR grants strong rights to access, delete, and object to data processing - AI-specific regulations (the EU AI Act) are rolling out - Schools and AI companies must comply if they serve EU users

In Canada, UK, Australia: - Similar privacy frameworks exist at varying levels of protection

Exercising Your Rights

You generally have the right to: 1. **Request your data** — ask the AI company for everything they hold about you 2. **Request deletion** — ask for your data to be deleted 3. **Opt out of data sale/sharing** — where law applies 4. **Know what data is collected** — companies must disclose their practices

The Bigger Picture

Privacy isn't about having something to hide. It's about keeping control over your personal information in a world where data is valuable and permanent.

The conversations you have with AI today could, in theory, sit on company servers indefinitely. The research ideas you share could land in a training dataset. The personal reflections you type could be reviewed by safety teams.

None of this means you shouldn't use AI. It means use it with awareness. Share what the task requires. Anonymize what you can. Opt out of training use when your platform allows it. Use institutional tools when available. And never share information that could cause real harm if exposed.

Students who treat AI as a private journal take unnecessary risks. Students who refuse AI on privacy grounds leave valuable tools on the table. The sweet spot — informed, intentional use with appropriate precautions — is where you want to be.

Be smart about what you share. Then use AI freely for everything else.

Chapter 17: When AI Gets It Wrong

The Confident Liar

AI has a problem no other tool you use shares: it sounds completely confident even when it's completely wrong. A calculator throws an error when you divide by zero. A search engine returns "no results found." Your textbook says "this is a simplified model" when it's leaving things out.

AI looks you straight in the eye — metaphorically — and tells you something utterly false with the same tone and certainty it uses for something perfectly true. And unlike a human who hesitates or hedges when unsure, AI often delivers fabricated information with more confidence than accurate information.

This isn't a minor inconvenience. If you use AI for academic work and don't verify what it tells you, you will eventually submit something wrong. A fabricated citation in a research paper. An incorrect formula in a problem set. A historical claim that never happened. And the consequences — a bad grade, an integrity investigation, or just looking foolish in front of a professor — fall on you, not on the AI.

This chapter teaches you how to catch AI's errors before they become your errors.

How AI Gets Things Wrong

Understanding why AI makes mistakes helps you predict when they're most likely.

Hallucinations

"Hallucination" is the term for AI generating information that sounds plausible but is entirely made up. This includes:

Fabricated citations. AI produces a reference that looks real — author name, journal title, year, volume, pages, even DOI — but the paper doesn't exist. The author might be real, the journal might be real, but that specific paper was never published.

This is the most dangerous hallucination for students because citations carry implicit authority. A citation in your paper tells the reader (and your professor) that you found this source, read it, and reported its findings accurately. A fabricated citation reveals that you did none of those things.

Fabricated facts. AI states something as fact that isn't true. "The Battle of Hastings took place in 1066" is correct. "The Battle of Hastings was the first use of cavalry in English warfare" might not be — and AI won't flag which statements are verified and which are generated.

Fabricated quotes. AI attributes statements to real people who never made them. Einstein said something about quantum computing. Shakespeare wrote a line that appears in none of his works.

Confident Incorrectness

Sometimes AI doesn't fabricate from scratch — it just gets things wrong:

Mathematical errors. AI can flub arithmetic, apply formulas incorrectly, or pick the wrong approach. This is particularly insidious: AI will show you "steps" that look correct but contain an error buried in the middle.

Logical errors. AI constructs arguments that feel logical but contain formal fallacies. It affirms the consequent, equivocates on terms, or draws conclusions that don't follow from the premises.

Outdated information. AI's training data has a cutoff. Events, policies, statistics, and facts that changed after that cutoff get reported incorrectly — and AI usually won't warn you its information might be stale.

Oversimplification. Explaining complex topics, AI sometimes simplifies to the point of inaccuracy. The explanation sounds clear and satisfying but misses crucial nuances your course actually cares about.

Pattern Matching Gone Wrong

AI generates text by predicting which words come next based on patterns in its training data. This means:

Common misconceptions get amplified. If a misconception shows up frequently in training data (even in contexts that debunk it), AI may present it as fact.

Majority views dominate. On genuinely contested topics, AI tends to present the most common perspective as the default, even when minority positions are well-supported.

Plausibility beats accuracy. A plausible-sounding wrong answer can be more "likely" (in the statistical sense AI uses) than an accurate but less common correct one.

What to Verify and How

The Verification Hierarchy

Not everything AI tells you needs the same level of scrutiny. Here's a practical hierarchy:

Always verify: - Specific citations (author, title, journal, year, DOI) - Statistical claims (numbers, percentages, study results) - Historical dates, events, and attributions - Quotes attributed to specific people - Legal or policy claims - Medical or safety information

Usually verify: - Definitions of technical terms (compare with your textbook) - Explanations of processes or mechanisms - Claims about "most researchers agree" or "the consensus is" - Comparisons between concepts

Spot-check: - General explanations of well-known concepts - Descriptions of widely documented events - Commonly taught material that matches your textbook

Trust with caution: - AI's analysis of text you've provided (it can still misinterpret) - AI's structural suggestions for your work - AI's feedback on your writing

How to Verify Citations

This is the most critical verification skill for students:

1. **Search the exact title** on Google Scholar, your library database, or the journal's website
2. **Check the DOI** by visiting doi.org/[the DOI AI gave you]
3. **Verify the author** — does this person exist and publish in this field?
4. **Check the journal** — is it real? Is it reputable?
5. **Read at least the abstract** — does the paper actually say what AI claims?

If any check fails, the citation is fabricated or inaccurate. Don't use it.

Tools for verification: - Google Scholar (scholar.google.com) - CrossRef (crossref.org) — verify DOIs - Your school's library databases - Semantic Scholar - The journal's own website

How to Verify Facts

1. **Cross-reference your textbook** — your course textbook is the primary authority for your coursework
2. **Check multiple independent sources** — if only AI says it, be suspicious
3. **Use Perplexity** — its real-time search with citations helps verify claims
4. **Check Wikipedia** — despite its reputation, Wikipedia's fact-checking often beats AI's claims on well-covered topics
5. **Ask your professor** — when in doubt, go to the expert

How to Verify Math

1. **Work through the steps yourself** — don't just check the final answer
2. **Use Wolfram Alpha** — it's a computational engine (not a language model) and its math is reliable
3. **Check units and dimensions** — if the units don't work out, the answer is wrong
4. **Test simple cases** — does the formula give the right answer for inputs where you already know it?
5. **Use your calculator** — for arithmetic, a calculator beats AI

Red Flags That AI Might Be Wrong

Learn to recognize warning signs:

Suspiciously specific details. A very precise number, date, or statistic with no hedging may be fabricated. Real academic knowledge often comes with uncertainty.

Too-perfect stories. An example or anecdote perfectly tailored to a point may be generated rather than real. Real examples tend to be messier.

Unfamiliar terminology used confidently. If AI uses a term you've never seen in your course material, verify that the term is actually used in the field.

Circular reasoning. If AI's explanation explains itself — the conclusion restates the premise — the reasoning is hollow.

Changing answers. Ask AI the same question twice and get different answers, and at least one is wrong. Especially common with math.

Excessive hedging on well-known topics. Conversely, if AI hedges heavily on something your textbook states flatly, the model may be uncertain for a reason worth investigating.

Building a Verification Habit

The goal is to make verification automatic — something you do without thinking:

The "Source or It Didn't Happen" Rule

For every factual claim AI makes that you plan to use in your work, find an independent source that confirms it. No confirmation, no citation.

AI may still be right — you just can't verify it. The academic standard is unforgiving here: if you can't verify it, you can't cite it.

The Three-Source Test

For important claims, verify with three independent sources: 1. AI's claim 2. Your textbook or course materials 3. A third independent source (academic database, authoritative website, peer-reviewed paper)

If all three agree, you can be confident. If they disagree, investigate further.

The "Explain It to Me Differently" Test

If you're unsure whether AI's explanation is correct, ask it to explain the same concept a different way. If the second explanation contradicts the first, something is wrong. If both are consistent and match your textbook, you're probably on solid ground.

```
You just explained [concept]. I want to make sure I understood correctly.
Can you explain it a completely different way, using a different analogy
or approach? Don't just rephrase - actually explain it differently.
```

The "What Are You Unsure About?" Prompt

Most AI models can flag their own uncertainty when you ask directly:

```
In your last response, how confident are you in each claim? Are there
any points where you might be wrong or where the evidence is mixed?
What should I verify independently?
```

AI's self-assessment isn't perfect, but it often surfaces genuine uncertainty the initial response glossed over.

Case Studies in AI Errors

The Fabricated Legal Citation

A law student used AI to find cases supporting a brief. AI returned six citations with detailed descriptions of holdings. Four of the six were fabricated — the cases didn't exist. The student submitted the brief without checking. The professor, who routinely verifies citations, failed the student on the assignment and filed an academic integrity complaint.

Lesson: Always verify citations. Always.

The Wrong Formula

An engineering student asked AI for help on a fluid dynamics problem. AI used the correct equation but applied it incorrectly — wrong variable for a specific parameter. The answer looked reasonable; the student submitted it. The error propagated through three subsequent calculations, leaving the final answer off by an order of magnitude.

Lesson: Verify not just the formula but every step of its application. Check that your answer makes physical sense.

The Confident Historical Error

A history student asked AI about the causes of a historical event. AI returned a clear, well-structured explanation built around a causal claim historians would call oversimplified to the point of being misleading. The student built a paper around the claim without consulting the assigned readings, which presented a more nuanced view.

Lesson: AI gives you the common-knowledge version, not the expert version. Your coursework expects the expert version.

The Plausible-But-Wrong Code

A CS student used AI to generate a sorting algorithm. The code ran without errors and produced correct output for the test cases. But it failed the professor's edge cases — empty arrays, arrays with one element, arrays with all identical elements. AI's implementation was almost correct but didn't handle boundary conditions.

Lesson: Code that passes test cases isn't necessarily correct. Test edge cases. Understand the logic.

A Healthier Relationship with AI's Limitations

The point of this chapter isn't to make you distrust AI — it's to help you calibrate your trust. AI is an extremely useful tool that happens to be unreliable in specific, predictable ways. Once you know those ways, you can compensate.

Think of GPS navigation. GPS is mostly accurate and incredibly useful. But you've probably had GPS tell you to turn onto a road that doesn't exist, navigate you to the wrong address, or route you through pointless detours. You don't stop using GPS — but you also don't drive into a lake because GPS told you to.

AI is the same. Use it. Trust the general direction. Verify the specifics. And keep enough independent knowledge to recognize when something doesn't smell right.

The student who treats AI as infallible will eventually get burned. The student who treats AI as useless leaves value on the table. The student who trusts but verifies gets the best of both worlds.

Be that student.

Part VII: Navigating AI in the Classroom

"Do not let schooling interfere with your education."

— Mark Twain (attributed)

Chapter 18: Working with Professors Who Ban AI

The No-AI Policy

You walk into class on the first day. The professor hands out the syllabus. Under "Academic Integrity," in bold: "The use of AI tools (including ChatGPT, Claude, Gemini, and similar platforms) is prohibited for all assignments in this course. Any use of AI-generated content will be treated as academic misconduct."

Your heart sinks. You've been using AI all semester in other classes. You've built study habits around it. Now you're expected to work without it.

This chapter is about handling that situation productively, respectfully, and successfully.

Why Professors Ban AI

Before you dismiss the policy as outdated or unfair, understand the reasons behind it. They aren't all wrong:

The Pedagogical Argument

Some skills only develop through struggle. A creative writing professor who bans AI isn't being a luddite — they're protecting the developmental process that turns a mediocre writer into a good one. That process requires writing badly, getting feedback, and writing less badly. AI short-circuits it by producing competent text before the student has developed competence.

The same logic applies to: - **Philosophy courses** where the point is constructing arguments from scratch - **Introductory courses** where foundational skills are being built - **Language courses** where immersion in struggle is how fluency develops - **Proof-based math courses** where formal reasoning requires doing it yourself

In these contexts, AI doesn't help you learn — it prevents you from learning by removing the productive struggle learning requires.

The Equity Argument

Not every student has equal access to AI tools. Some can afford ChatGPT Plus; others can't. Some have reliable internet; others don't. Some have the digital literacy to use AI effectively; others don't.

A professor who bans AI may be trying to ensure all students compete on the same playing field. Whether that's the right approach is debatable, but the concern is legitimate.

The Assessment Argument

Professors need to know what YOU can do, not what you and AI can do together. If AI is allowed, the professor can't distinguish a student who understands the material from one who knows how to prompt AI effectively. For courses where individual competence matters — prerequisites, foundational skills courses, capstones — this is a valid concern.

The Practical Argument

Some professors aren't opposed to AI in principle — they just haven't worked out how to design assignments that incorporate AI while still assessing student learning. Rather than do it badly, they ban it until they figure it out. That's a reasonable position.

The Wrong Reasons

Let's be honest: some professors ban AI because they're uncomfortable with technology, resistant to change, or haven't thought carefully about the issue. They may conflate all AI use with cheating, or see AI as an existential threat to their discipline.

Even when the reasoning is flawed, the policy still applies. You won't change their mind by arguing, and you won't benefit from violating the policy.

Respecting the Policy

This is straightforward: if the syllabus says no AI, don't use AI for that course's submitted work.

Not "use AI and rephrase the output." Not "use AI for research and write it yourself." Not "just a little." If the policy says no AI, the expectation is no AI.

Why this matters beyond the obvious risk of getting caught:

You agreed to it. By enrolling and receiving the syllabus, you've implicitly agreed to the course policies. Breaking them isn't civil disobedience — it's contract violation.

The consequences are severe. Academic integrity violations can mean failing grades, suspension, or expulsion. They follow you. Graduate schools ask about them. Professional licensing boards ask about them. It's not worth it.

You can learn without AI. Students earned excellent grades for centuries before AI existed. The tools in AI's absence are the same ones that built every expert in every field: reading carefully, thinking hard, writing repeatedly, studying actively, and asking humans for help.

Thriving Without AI

The absence of AI isn't a handicap — it's a different mode of working. How to succeed in no-AI courses:

Study Techniques That Don't Require AI

Everything in Chapter 7 about effective studying has non-AI equivalents:

Active recall without AI: - Physical flashcards (index cards are cheap and effective) - Anki or Quizlet (study tools, not AI generators — check whether your professor's policy covers them) - Cover your notes and try to recall the key points - Study with a partner and quiz each other

Spaced repetition without AI: - Build a study schedule manually (or use a spaced repetition app like Anki) - Review material at increasing intervals using your calendar

Practice problems without AI: - Your textbook's problem sets - Other textbooks at your library - Ask your professor for extra practice problems - Study groups where members write practice questions for each other

Writing Without AI

```
[In your own head, not in an AI chatbot:]
```

Brainstorming: Freewrite for ten minutes on your topic. Don't worry about quality — get ideas on paper. Use mind maps. Talk your ideas through with a friend.

Outlining: Organize your brainstormed ideas into a logical structure. Move things around. Ask yourself: if I could only make three points, what would they be?

Drafting: Write the draft. It will be rough. Fine. A bad draft is infinitely more useful than no draft.

Revising: Read your draft out loud. Mark every place where you stumble — those are clarity problems. Show the draft to a friend, a writing tutor, or your school's writing center.

Editing: Read backward, sentence by sentence, for grammar and mechanics. Use spell-check — universally allowed, even in no-AI classrooms.

Research Without AI

The research tools that predate AI still work:

- **Google Scholar** for finding academic papers
- **Your library databases** (JSTOR, PubMed, etc.) for full-text access
- **Reference librarians** — genuinely underused. They're experts at finding information. Visit the reference desk.
- **Your textbook's bibliography** — curated starting points
- **Citation chasing** — find one good paper, then look at what it cites and who has cited it

Getting Help from Humans

Without AI, human support networks matter more:

Office hours. Office hours exist for exactly this purpose. Show up with specific questions. Professors are more helpful when you can say "I'm stuck on step 3 of this problem" rather than "I don't understand anything."

Teaching assistants. TAs are often closer to your level and can explain things in more accessible ways.

Tutoring centers. Most schools offer free tutoring. Use it.

Writing centers. Free writing feedback from trained peers. They won't write your paper, but they'll help you improve it.

Study groups. Explaining concepts to each other is one of the most effective learning techniques. Form groups. Meet regularly.

Classmates. Ask questions. Share notes. Discuss readings. Informal academic conversation is irreplaceable.

What to Do When the Policy Is Unclear

Sometimes the AI policy is vaguely worded or doesn't cover your case. For example: - The policy says "no AI-generated content" but you want to use AI to explain a concept (not generate content) - The policy says "no ChatGPT" but doesn't mention other tools - The policy doesn't address AI at all — there's no mention of it

The Default Rule

When the policy is unclear, default to the most restrictive reasonable interpretation. If you're unsure whether something is allowed, assume it isn't. That keeps you safe.

Ask

Send a brief, respectful email:

```
Subject: Quick question about AI policy for [Assignment Name]

Professor [Name],

I want to make sure I understand the AI policy for this course. The
syllabus states [quote the policy]. I wanted to confirm: does this
apply to using AI to [specific use you're considering]? I want to
make sure I'm in full compliance.
```

```
Thank you,
[Your name]
```

This email does several things at once: - Shows you read the syllabus - Shows you care about integrity - Gets you a clear answer - Protects you (written confirmation of what's allowed)

When You Disagree with the Policy

You might genuinely believe AI should be allowed in a course. You might think the ban is counterproductive, outdated, or unreasonable. You might be right.

Here's what to do about it:

Constructive Approaches

Engage when invited. If your professor opens a discussion about AI policy, share your perspective thoughtfully. Focus on learning outcomes, not convenience. "I think AI could help us engage more deeply with the material by [specific way]" beats "Everyone uses AI anyway."

Use official channels. End-of-course evaluations are the right place to suggest policy changes. Be specific and constructive: "I would have benefited from being allowed to use AI for [specific purpose] because [learning reason]."

Talk to your department. If you feel strongly that AI policy should change, engage with student government, departmental committees, or academic policy bodies. Institutional change happens through institutional channels.

Counterproductive Approaches

Don't argue in class. Publicly challenging a professor's policy in front of other students puts them on the defensive and rarely changes anything.

Don't use AI anyway and hope you don't get caught. The risk-reward is terrible. The potential cost (integrity violation, failing grade) dwarfs the benefit (saving time on one assignment).

Don't use AI and then lie about it. Lying when asked directly turns a bad situation catastrophically worse. An integrity violation plus dishonesty in an investigation is the fastest path to severe consequences.

Don't assume future professors will be the same. Each professor sets their own policy. Don't carry resentment from one course into another.

The Silver Lining

Working without AI in some courses has genuine benefits:

You prove you can do it. In job interviews, nobody cares that you can prompt AI well if you can't also demonstrate independent competence. AI-free courses build that proof.

You develop foundational skills. Writing a clean first draft, debugging code manually, solving problems without hints, researching without AI — these foundational skills make you better at using AI later, because you understand what AI is actually doing.

You appreciate AI more. After writing a research paper without AI, you'll have a much clearer sense of where AI saves real time and where it's a distraction. That calibration makes you a more effective AI user.

You build resilience. AI tools go down. Subscriptions lapse. Internet fails during power outages. The student who can only work with AI is stuck in those moments. The student who can work with or without AI keeps moving.

The Bottom Line

A no-AI policy isn't an obstacle — it's a constraint, and working within constraints is a professional skill. Every engineer works within material constraints. Every writer works within word limits. Every businessperson works within budgets.

You'll encounter no-AI environments throughout your career — secure environments, organizations with AI restrictions, situations where the stakes are too high to risk AI errors. Producing excellent work without AI is a competitive advantage, not a handicap.

Respect the policy. Use the course to build skills you'll have forever. Save your AI tools for the courses and contexts where they're welcome.

Chapter 19: Working with Professors Who Encourage AI

The Open Door

Some professors don't just allow AI — they encourage it. They design assignments that require AI use, teach you how to prompt effectively, and treat your ability to work with AI as a skill in its own right. These courses point toward the future of education, and they're your best chance to develop AI competencies that will serve you professionally.

An AI-friendly classroom isn't a free pass. The expectations are different, not lower. Courses that encourage AI often hold the final product to a higher bar — the professor knows you had AI assistance.

This chapter is about getting the most out of AI-friendly courses.

Understanding AI-Encouraging Policies

AI-friendly courses typically fall into a few categories:

AI Required

Some courses require AI. Most common in: - Computer science courses teaching AI integration - Business courses on AI strategy and applications - Data science and analytics courses - Advanced writing courses focused on AI-assisted composition - Digital humanities courses

Assignments are designed around AI, and your grade depends partly on how well you wield it.

AI Encouraged with Disclosure

The most common AI-friendly policy: use AI for any or all of your work, but document what you used and how. The disclosure becomes part of the assignment.

This approach treats AI as part of the modern toolkit while demanding transparency. Your professor can then assess not just your output but your process — how thoughtfully you used AI, where you added original thinking, what judgment you exercised.

AI as a Learning Objective

Some courses teach AI skills directly: effective prompting, critical evaluation of AI output, understanding AI limitations, ethical AI use. In these courses, your AI competency is directly assessed.

AI Optional but Welcome

The most relaxed policy: use AI if you want, don't if you don't, no disclosure required. Maximum flexibility — and maximum responsibility for making good choices.

Exceeding Expectations in AI-Friendly Courses

When AI is allowed, everyone has the same tools. The differentiator isn't whether you use AI — it's how.

The Minimum vs. the Maximum

The minimum: Use AI to generate work, submit it, disclose that you used AI. This meets the policy. It earns a mediocre grade because the professor can see AI did the heavy lifting and you did the light editing.

The maximum: Use AI to elevate your work beyond what either you or AI could produce alone. That means:

1. **Starting with your own thinking** before involving AI
2. **Using AI to challenge and refine** rather than generate
3. **Adding analysis and insight** AI can't produce
4. **Exercising judgment** about what to keep, what to change, what to reject from AI's output
5. **Producing work that clearly shows** a human mind directing AI capability

The best work in AI-friendly courses doesn't look AI-generated. It looks like the work of a smart, well-prepared student who had really good tools at their disposal.

The Process Documentation

When disclosure is required, treat it as a chance to showcase your thinking:

Weak disclosure: "I used ChatGPT to help write this paper."

Strong disclosure:

```
AI Use Documentation:

Research Phase:
- Used Perplexity to identify initial sources on [topic]. Found 8
  relevant papers, of which 5 were included in my final bibliography
  after reading and evaluation.
- Used Claude to help me understand the methodology in [Author]'s
  paper, which uses [complex technique] I hadn't encountered before.

Writing Phase:
- Brainstormed thesis directions with ChatGPT. It suggested 4 angles;
  I chose to pursue [my thesis] because [reasoning].
- Wrote my first draft without AI. Used Claude to review my argument
  structure. It identified a logical gap between paragraphs 3 and 4,
  which I addressed by adding [what I added].
- Used Grammarly for proofreading.

What AI did NOT do:
- My thesis and analysis are my own
- All primary source analysis is my own reading and interpretation
- The comparative framework in Section 3 is original
```

This kind of disclosure shows intellectual maturity, clear thinking about AI's role in your work, and genuine engagement with the material. Professors notice.

Going Beyond the Assignment

In AI-friendly courses, you have headroom for more ambitious work:

```
[To yourself, when planning:]
What would I write for this assignment without AI?
What can I write WITH AI that goes significantly beyond that?
How can I use AI to reach a level of analysis or coverage that
would otherwise require weeks of additional work?
```

For example: - A literature review that covers twice as many sources because AI helped you triage and understand them (you still read the key ones yourself) - A data analysis that explores additional variables because AI helped you set up the statistical tests - A paper that handles counterarguments more thoroughly because AI surfaced ones you hadn't considered

Effective Prompting for Coursework

AI-friendly courses reward good prompting — the skill of communicating with AI effectively. Advanced prompting strategies:

The Context-Rich Prompt

```
I'm writing a paper for [specific course] taught by [professor name]
at the [undergraduate/graduate] level. The assignment asks me to
[assignment requirements]. The class has focused on [key themes and
frameworks from the course].

My thesis is [your thesis]. I've organized my paper as follows:
[your outline]

I need help with [specific aspect – argument development, finding
counterexamples, improving my introduction, etc.].

Important context:
- We've discussed [relevant class discussions or readings]
- My professor values [what they emphasize – original analysis?
  interdisciplinary connections? methodological rigor?]
- I want to avoid [common pitfalls for this type of assignment]
```

The more context you provide, the more useful AI's help becomes.

The Iterative Refinement

Don't accept AI's first response. Iterate:

1. Get an initial response
2. Identify what's useful and what isn't
3. Push back on weak points: "This part is too generic. Be more specific about [aspect]."
4. Challenge the AI's assumptions: "You're assuming [X]. What if [Y]?"
5. Ask for alternatives: "Give me three other ways to approach this."

6. Synthesize the best elements into your own work

The Role-Based Prompt

```
I want you to evaluate my work from three different perspectives:

1. As a professor grading against this rubric: [rubric]
2. As a skeptical peer reviewer who disagrees with my thesis
3. As a general reader who knows nothing about the topic

For each perspective, tell me what works, what doesn't, and what
specific changes would make the biggest difference.
```

The Constraint Prompt

```
Help me improve this [paper/analysis/code], but with these constraints:
- My thesis cannot change (it's already approved by my professor)
- I need to use only the sources I've already cited (I can't add new ones)
- The paper cannot exceed [word count]
- The tone must be [academic/professional/conversational]

Within these constraints, what are the highest-impact improvements
I can make?
```

Common Mistakes in AI-Friendly Courses

Over-Reliance

The most common mistake: because AI is allowed, students use it for everything and develop nothing. They produce decent work but can't discuss their own papers in class, can't answer questions about their analysis, and can't demonstrate the understanding the work is supposed to reflect.

Professors in AI-friendly courses often: - Require in-class presentations or defenses of written work - Ask oral follow-up questions about submitted assignments - Include in-class assessments that mirror take-home work

If your AI-assisted paper earns an A but you can't discuss it coherently in class, the disconnect gets noticed.

Lazy Disclosure

"I used AI" is not useful disclosure. Professors who require documentation want to see your thinking, not a checkbox. Weak disclosure suggests you don't understand your own work well enough to describe how you produced it.

Uniform AI Voice

When everyone in the class uses the same AI tool with similar prompts, submissions start to sound alike. Professors spot it immediately — 20 papers with the same structure, the same transitions, the same tone. To stand out: - Write your first draft yourself - Use AI for refinement, not generation - Keep your own writing voice - Bring course-specific insights AI can't access

Ignoring AI Errors

In AI-friendly courses, you own AI's mistakes. If AI gives you a wrong citation and you include it, you didn't verify your work — that's on you, not on AI. The verification standard from Chapter 17 matters even more when AI use is expected.

Making the Most of Explicit AI Instruction

If your course teaches AI skills directly, engage fully:

Prompt Engineering Practice

When your professor teaches prompting techniques, practice them beyond the assignments. Build a personal library of effective prompts for different academic tasks. The prompts in this book are starting points — adapt them to your courses, professors, and disciplines.

Critical Evaluation Skills

Courses that teach AI use also teach AI evaluation — how to spot when AI is wrong, biased, or unhelpful. Critical evaluation is one of the most valuable skills you can learn. It applies not just to AI but to every information source.

Ethical Frameworks

AI-friendly courses often include explicit discussion of AI ethics in academic and professional contexts. Engage with these discussions seriously. The ethical frameworks you build now will guide your professional AI use for years.

Building Your AI Portfolio

AI-friendly courses give you a chance to build evidence of AI competency:

Save your process documentation. The disclosure statements you write demonstrate professional-level AI use. Keep them.

Save effective prompts. Build a personal prompt library organized by task type. It becomes a professional resource.

Reflect on what you learned. After each AI-friendly course, write a brief reflection: what worked, what didn't, what would you do differently? Metacognitive practice accelerates learning.

Articulate your AI skills. On your resume, describe AI competency developed in these courses. "Developed AI-assisted research methodologies" or "Trained in AI-augmented data analysis" are legitimate skills employers value.

The Bridge to Professional AI Use

AI-friendly courses are the closest thing in education to how you'll use AI professionally. In the workplace, AI use is expected, documentation is often required, and the standard is results — not whether you used AI, but whether you produced excellent work with good judgment.

The habits you build in AI-friendly courses — thoughtful prompting, critical evaluation, transparent documentation, human-AI collaboration — transfer directly to professional contexts. Students who've learned to use AI well in academic settings consistently outperform those who either avoided AI entirely or used it as a crutch.

Take these courses seriously. They're teaching you a skill that will define professional competency for the rest of your career.

Advocating for More AI-Friendly Policies

If you benefit from AI-friendly courses and want more of them:

- Give specific, constructive feedback in course evaluations
- Share positive outcomes with other professors when appropriate
- Join institutional conversations about AI policy
- Help other students use AI responsibly (the rising tide lifts all boats)

The more students who use AI responsibly and produce better work because of it, the more professors will open their courses to AI use. Your behavior in AI-friendly courses sets the standard for students who come after you.

Be the example that makes professors say "this is working."

Part VIII: Your AI Future

"The future belongs to those who learn more skills and combine them in creative ways."

— Robert Greene

Chapter 20: Building AI Skills for Your Career

The Skill That Matters Most

Here's a prediction I'll make: within five years of your graduation, AI proficiency will be as expected in the workplace as spreadsheet proficiency is today. Not a specialty, not a differentiator — a baseline requirement across nearly every professional role.

The students who learn to use AI effectively right now — not just as a homework helper, but as a professional tool — will enter the workforce with a real competitive advantage. This chapter translates your academic AI experience into career-ready skills.

What Employers Actually Want

Let's start with what the job market looks like in 2026 for graduates with AI skills:

The Universal Skills

Regardless of your major, employers look for:

AI-augmented communication. Writing better emails, reports, proposals, and presentations with AI assistance. This doesn't mean letting AI write for you — it means using AI to produce faster, clearer, more polished communication.

AI-assisted research and analysis. Finding information, synthesizing sources, analyzing data, generating insights with AI support. Every knowledge worker does this; AI makes it faster and more thorough.

Critical evaluation of AI output. Distinguishing good AI output from bad, verifying claims, spotting when AI is wrong, and knowing when human judgment is needed. This may be the most important AI skill, because it separates competent users from people who blindly trust machines.

Prompt engineering. Communicating effectively with AI tools — framing questions clearly, supplying context, iterating on responses, and getting consistently useful results. The skill improves with practice and transfers across every AI platform.

Industry-Specific Applications

Beyond universal skills, specific industries have specific AI needs:

Business and finance: AI for market analysis, financial modeling, report generation, customer insights, competitive intelligence, and strategic planning.

Healthcare: AI for clinical decision support, medical literature review, patient communication, documentation, and research. Note: healthcare carries strict regulations around AI use that you'll need to understand.

Law: AI for legal research, contract analysis, case law review, document drafting, and compliance monitoring. Note: the legal profession is still establishing norms around AI use — adoption varies widely from firm to firm.

Engineering and technology: AI for code generation, system design, debugging, documentation, testing, and technical communication.

Marketing and communications: AI for content creation, campaign analysis, audience research, brand messaging, and social media strategy.

Education: AI for curriculum design, personalized learning, assessment creation, and student support. The irony: the institution most conflicted about AI is producing the graduates who'll use it most.

Creative industries: AI for ideation, design prototyping, content editing, research, and production workflows.

Translating Academic AI Use to Professional Skills

The AI skills you're building as a student map directly to professional competencies:

Academic Skill	Professional Equivalent
Using AI to understand course material	Using AI to get up to speed on new projects

Academic Skill	Professional Equivalent
AI-assisted research for papers	AI-assisted market research, competitive analysis
Using AI to improve your writing	Using AI to write reports, proposals, emails
AI for study and exam prep	AI for professional certification prep
Verifying AI output against textbooks	Verifying AI output against industry standards
AI-assisted data analysis for labs	AI-assisted business analytics
Disclosing AI use in assignments	Documenting AI use per company policy
Working within professor AI policies	Working within company AI policies

Building Your AI Resume

Demonstrable Skills

When you apply for jobs, demonstrate AI skills, don't just claim them. Here's how to build evidence:

Portfolio projects: Create projects that showcase your AI-augmented work. If you wrote a research paper where AI helped you cover twice as many sources, that's a portfolio piece — include the process documentation showing how you used AI.

Course projects: AI-friendly courses (Chapter 19) give you ready-made portfolio pieces. Save your best work, with the process documentation.

Personal projects: Use AI to build something outside of class — a blog, a small application, a research project, a business plan. Show that you can self-direct AI use toward productive outcomes.

Certifications: AI-specific certifications are still maturing, but Google, Microsoft, and various online learning providers offer courses and certifications in AI applications. These carry varying weight but show initiative.

How to Talk About AI Skills in Interviews

Don't say: "I'm good with AI" or "I use ChatGPT a lot."

Do say: - "I developed a systematic research process using AI tools that let me synthesize literature from multiple disciplines for my thesis." - "I used AI to identify weaknesses in my analytical frameworks, then addressed those weaknesses with original research." - "I built workflows that combined AI-assisted drafting with rigorous human review, producing higher-quality deliverables in less time." - "I have experience evaluating AI output for accuracy and judging when to trust the analysis versus when to verify independently."

These descriptions show sophistication, judgment, and process — not just tool usage.

Interview Preparation with AI

Use AI to prep for interviews where AI skills might come up:

```
I'm interviewing for a [position] at [company/industry]. They'll
likely ask about my AI skills. Help me prepare:

1. What AI-related questions are common for [industry] interviews?
2. How do I describe my AI experience in terms that resonate with
   hiring managers?
3. What are the AI tools and practices most relevant to [industry]?
4. What questions should I ask the interviewer about the company's
   AI adoption?
5. How do I demonstrate AI judgment (knowing when to use AI and
   when not to) rather than just AI usage?
```

AI Skills by Major

For Business and Economics Majors

The business world has adopted AI faster than almost any other sector. Skills to build:

- Using AI for market analysis and competitive research
- AI-assisted financial modeling and scenario planning
- Generating executive summaries and board-ready reports
- Using AI to analyze customer data and identify trends
- Automating routine business writing (emails, memos, updates)
- Understanding AI's limitations in strategic decision-making

Practice project: Use AI to analyze a real company's annual report, identify key trends, and produce an investor-ready summary.

For STEM Majors

Technical AI skills are the most directly employable:

- Writing and debugging code with AI assistance
- Using AI for data analysis and visualization
- AI-assisted technical documentation
- Understanding AI/ML concepts at a functional level
- Evaluating AI tools for technical accuracy
- Building AI-enhanced workflows and automations

Practice project: Build a small application that integrates an AI API (OpenAI's or Anthropic's) for a practical purpose.

For Humanities and Social Sciences Majors

Don't assume AI is only for tech roles. Humanities graduates with AI literacy are in demand:

- AI-assisted policy analysis and research
- Content strategy with AI support
- Qualitative data analysis with AI tools
- AI-enhanced archival and historical research
- Ethical AI evaluation (a growing field that values humanities training)
- AI-assisted communications and media analysis

Practice project: Use AI to analyze public policy documents and produce an accessible summary for a general audience, with critical analysis of the policy's implications.

For Pre-Professional Students (Pre-Med, Pre-Law, Education)

Professional schools increasingly value AI competency:

- Understanding AI's role in your future profession
- Ethical considerations of AI in professional practice

- AI for professional exam preparation
- Using AI within the regulatory framework of your field
- Staying current with AI developments in your profession

Practice project: Research how AI is currently used in your target profession and write a brief analysis of the opportunities and risks.

The AI Literacy Spectrum

Think of AI competency as a spectrum:

Level 1: AI User — You use AI tools for basic tasks (asking questions, generating text, getting information). Most students are here.

Level 2: AI Practitioner — You use AI strategically, pick the right tool for the right task, verify output, and integrate AI into complex workflows. This is where this book aims to get you.

Level 3: AI Integrator — You design workflows that combine AI with other tools and human processes. You understand AI's strengths and limitations deeply enough to make architectural decisions about where AI belongs and where it doesn't.

Level 4: AI Builder — You build applications and systems that use AI APIs, fine-tune models for specific tasks, and ship AI-powered products. This requires technical skills beyond what most non-CS students develop.

For most professionals, Level 2–3 is the sweet spot. Level 4 is for those pursuing technical AI careers specifically.

Professional AI Norms

Company AI Policies

Just as schools have AI policies, so do companies — and theirs are often stricter:

- **Data handling:** Companies deal with customer data, proprietary information, trade secrets, and regulated data. You may not be able to paste company data into public AI tools.

- **Approved tools:** Many companies restrict AI use to approved platforms that meet their security and privacy requirements.
- **Disclosure requirements:** Some industries (legal, financial, healthcare) require disclosure of AI use in client-facing work.
- **Quality standards:** AI-assisted work may need to clear specific review and approval processes.

The habits you build around responsible AI use in school — verifying output, respecting policies, disclosing use, protecting sensitive information — transfer directly to professional contexts.

The Professional Integrity Standard

In professional life, the integrity standard shifts from "did you do the work yourself?" to "is the work correct, appropriate, and well-judged?" Nobody in a corporate setting cares whether AI helped you write a report. They care whether the report is accurate, well-reasoned, and useful.

The underlying principle still holds: you are responsible for the work you deliver. If AI generates an error and you submit it, it's your error. If AI produces a biased analysis and you don't catch it, it's your failure. Professional AI use demands the same verification habits you're building now.

Staying Current

AI is moving fast. The tools and techniques you learn today will change. The principles won't, but the implementations will. Here's how to stay current after graduation:

Follow the platforms. Subscribe to update blogs from OpenAI, Anthropic, Google, and other major AI providers. Major releases and feature changes happen multiple times per year.

Professional development. Attend workshops, webinars, and conferences on AI in your industry. Most professional associations now include AI tracks.

Experimentation. When a new AI tool or feature launches, try it. Build your own evaluation criteria: is this genuinely useful for my work, or is it hype?

Community. Join professional communities (LinkedIn groups, Slack channels, industry forums) focused on AI in your field. Learning from peers is one of the fastest ways to stay current.

Reading. Books like this one will have new editions as the landscape evolves. The AI for Everyone series tracks changes across the AI ecosystem.

The Mindset Shift

The most important career-related AI skill isn't technical — it's attitudinal. It's the ability to treat AI as a tool that amplifies your capabilities, not a threat to your relevance or a crutch that replaces your skills.

The professionals who struggle with AI either refuse to learn it (and fall behind) or rely on it uncritically (and make expensive mistakes). The ones who thrive develop the judgment to use AI where it helps and their own expertise where it's needed.

You're building that judgment right now — in every course, with every assignment, through every interaction with AI tools. The academic exercises are practice for the real thing.

When you graduate and enter the workforce, you won't just be someone who "knows how to use ChatGPT." You'll be someone who knows how to think alongside AI — when to trust it, when to question it, how to direct it, and how to produce work that's better than either you or AI could create alone.

That skill will serve you for your entire career. Start building it now.

Chapter 21: The Future of AI in Education

What's Coming

Predicting the future of technology is a fool's errand. Nobody in 2020 predicted that by 2023, every student would have access to an AI that could write essays. Nobody in 2023 predicted how quickly institutions would adapt — or how chaotically.

But we can identify trends already in motion and think about where they're heading. This chapter isn't speculation. It's extrapolation from what's already happening, aimed at helping you prepare for the educational and professional landscape you'll inhabit over the next five to ten years.

Trend 1: Personalized AI Tutoring

Where We Are

Today, AI tutoring is conversational — you ask questions and get answers. Powerful but generic. The AI doesn't know what you learned yesterday, what you chronically struggle with, what grade you're aiming for, or how you learn best. Every conversation starts from scratch.

Where We're Heading

AI tutoring systems will become persistent and personalized. Imagine an AI that:

- Knows your entire academic history and current courseload
- Tracks what concepts you've mastered and which you haven't
- Adjusts its teaching style based on what works for you specifically
- Remembers you learned integration by parts three weeks ago and tests your retention at spaced intervals
- Spots when you're about to hit a concept that requires a prerequisite you're shaky on, and addresses that proactively

This isn't hypothetical. Early versions of personalized AI tutoring already exist — Khan Academy's Khanmigo is one example. Over the next few years, these systems will get dramatically more capable.

What This Means for You

The students who engage with personalized AI tutors thoughtfully — giving honest feedback about their understanding, not gaming the system — will learn faster and more effectively. The students who find ways to make the AI think they understand when they don't will rack up larger and larger knowledge gaps.

The same integrity principles from Chapter 3 apply, but the stakes change. When an AI tutor knows your weaknesses, the temptation to look more competent than you are is both stronger and more destructive.

Trend 2: AI-Adapted Assessment

Where We Are

Most assessment still follows the traditional model: everyone gets the same exam, the same essay prompt, the same problem set. AI has made this model partially obsolete because the tasks can be outsourced to AI — but the alternative, personalized adaptive assessment, is still emerging.

Where We're Heading

Assessment will become more personalized, more frequent, and less dependent on high-stakes exams:

Adaptive testing. Exams that adjust difficulty in real time based on your responses. Answer a hard question correctly and the next one gets harder. Miss an easy one and the test probes to find exactly where your understanding breaks down. The result: a more accurate measurement of competency in less time.

Process-based assessment. Instead of grading only your final paper, professors will increasingly grade your process — research documentation, revision history, AI interaction logs, thinking progression. Much harder to fake competence; much easier to demonstrate genuine learning.

Competency-based progression. Rather than everyone moving through a course at the same pace, some programs will let you advance when you demonstrate mastery and provide extra support when you don't. AI makes this practical by delivering personalized assessment at scale.

Authentic assessment. Assignments designed to resist AI outsourcing — presentations with Q&A, in-class application exercises, portfolios developed over time, collaborative projects with individual accountability.

What This Means for You

The shift toward process-based and competency-based assessment is good news if you've been using AI responsibly. Your documentation habits, your ability to explain your thinking, and your genuine understanding become your strongest assets. Students who used AI as a shortcut will find it harder to hide.

Trend 3: AI-Enhanced Course Design

Where We Are

Most courses are still designed the way they've been designed for decades: syllabus, lectures, readings, assessments. AI is bolted on as an afterthought, if at all.

Where We're Heading

Course design will increasingly be built around AI from the start:

AI-informed curricula. Departments will use data from AI tutoring systems to identify where students consistently struggle and redesign curricula around those pain points. Courses will get more responsive to actual student needs.

Dynamic reading lists. Instead of static lists, courses may use AI to recommend readings tailored to each student's interests and knowledge gaps.

Hybrid AI-human instruction. Lectures for foundational content (where AI can supplement), with class time reserved for discussion, application, and the human interactions AI can't replicate. The flipped classroom, powered by AI.

Real-time course adjustment. Professors will get aggregated data about where students are struggling — from AI tutoring interactions, adaptive assessments, and similar sources — and can adjust their teaching in real time.

Trend 4: Credential and Skill Verification

Where We Are

Degrees are the primary credential. They verify that you completed a program, not that you retained specific skills.

Where We're Heading

The value of credentials will shift from "time spent" to "competency demonstrated":

Micro-credentials and badges. Verifiable evidence of specific skills – "proficient in statistical analysis using R," "competent in AI-assisted research methodology," "demonstrated proficiency in academic writing." These complement degrees with granular skill information.

Continuous assessment. Instead of testing once and moving on, critical skills may require periodic re-verification. Already standard in medicine (continuing education) and spreading to other fields.

Portfolio-based evidence. Employers will increasingly look at portfolios of actual work rather than relying on GPA or degree prestige. Your documented AI-assisted projects become career assets.

Proctored skill demonstrations. For high-stakes credentials, expect more in-person or proctored demonstrations – environments where you can't use AI, proving the skills are genuinely yours.

What This Means for You

Building genuine skills matters more than ever. Credentials will get better at distinguishing students who understand the material from students who passed courses. The trend is toward more, not less, accountability for actual competence.

Trend 5: AI Literacy as a Core Requirement

Where We Are

AI literacy is mostly self-taught or limited to specific courses. There's no universal standard for what students should know about AI.

Where We're Heading

AI literacy will become a core educational requirement, similar to computer literacy in the 2000s:

Required AI courses. Many universities already require AI literacy courses for all students, not just CS majors. These cover effective use, limitations, ethics, and critical evaluation.

AI across the curriculum. Just as writing across the curriculum became standard decades ago, AI across the curriculum will follow. Every course will address how AI relates to its discipline.

K–12 AI education. AI literacy will move into high school and eventually middle school curricula. Students entering college in 2030 will arrive with far more AI experience than students entering today.

Standardized AI competency frameworks. Institutions and accrediting bodies will develop standardized expectations for AI literacy at different educational levels.

What This Means for You

If you're reading this book, you're ahead of the curve. The skills and frameworks here will become standard expectations within a few years. Early adopters who build thoughtful AI practices now will be the leaders and mentors later.

Trend 6: The Changing Role of Professors

Where We Are

Professors are primarily lecturers, assignment designers, and evaluators.

Where We're Heading

As AI absorbs some of these functions, the professorial role will shift toward:

Mentorship and coaching. The distinctly human parts of education — motivation, career guidance, intellectual development, professional socialization — become more central when AI handles content delivery.

Critical discussion leadership. AI can deliver information, but it can't lead a Socratic seminar, push students to deeper thinking through live dialogue, or build the intellectual community that defines great education.

Research supervision. Guiding students through original research demands judgment, creativity, and domain expertise that AI supports but doesn't replace.

Ethical formation. Teaching students not just how to do things but whether they should — the ethical and philosophical dimensions that grow more important as AI makes more things possible.

Trend 7: Global Access and Equity

Where We Are

Access to quality education is wildly unequal, both within and between countries.

Where We're Heading

AI has the potential to democratize education in unprecedented ways:

Free, high-quality tutoring for everyone. A student in rural India can access the same AI tutor as a student at Stanford. The knowledge gap narrows.

Language barriers reduced. Real-time translation and multilingual AI make educational content accessible across languages.

Accessibility improvements. AI assistive technologies (Chapter 14) will keep getting more sophisticated, making education more accessible for students with disabilities.

But also: digital divides may widen. Students with better internet, newer devices, and paid AI subscriptions will have advantages. The equity questions from Chapter 1 don't go away — they intensify.

What Won't Change

Amid all this change, some things are durable:

Learning requires effort. No AI will ever make learning effortless. Understanding is built through struggle, practice, and engagement. The tools change; the cognitive processes don't.

Integrity matters. The specific forms will evolve, but the fundamental principle — that your credentials should reflect your actual capabilities — will hold.

Human judgment is irreplaceable. AI will get better at many tasks, but making value judgments, weighing competing priorities, navigating ambiguity, and leading other humans demand distinctly human capabilities.

Relationships are central. The best parts of education — the professor who changed how you think, the study group that became lifelong friends, the research mentor who shaped your career — are irreducibly human.

Deep expertise takes time. AI makes surface knowledge more accessible, which makes deep expertise more valuable, not less. The person who truly understands a field — its nuances, its history, its debates, its unsolved problems — brings something AI can't.

Preparing for the Unknown

The honest answer to "what will AI in education look like in 2030?" is "we don't know." But we can prepare for uncertainty by building skills robust across different futures:

Adaptability. Learning new tools quickly. You won't be using the same AI platforms in five years that you're using today. Picking up new tools, evaluating them critically, and integrating them into your workflow matters more than mastery of any specific tool.

Critical thinking. Evaluating information, constructing arguments, spotting biases, and making reasoned judgments. The human counterpart to AI's computational power.

Communication. Explaining complex ideas clearly, persuading diverse audiences, and collaborating with both humans and AI systems. AI makes this more important, not less.

Ethical reasoning. Navigating complex ethical situations where the rules haven't been written yet. AI creates new ethical questions faster than institutions create policies.

Self-directed learning. Identifying what you need to learn and figuring out how to learn it. In a rapidly changing landscape, nobody hands you a syllabus for what you need to know next.

Your Role in Shaping the Future

You're not just a passive recipient of whatever AI future arrives. You have agency:

As a student: Your choices about how to use AI responsibly shape institutional policies. When students demonstrate thoughtful AI use, institutions open up. When students misuse AI, institutions lock down.

As a professional: The norms you establish in your workplace — how AI is used, how its limitations are managed, how quality is maintained — shape your industry's AI culture.

As a citizen: The policies, regulations, and social norms governing AI in education and society are shaped by public participation. Your informed perspective as someone who has actually used AI in education matters in these conversations.

As a future educator or mentor: Whether or not you teach professionally, you'll mentor and teach throughout your career. The AI literacy you develop now will shape how you help others learn.

The Choice

The future of AI in education will be shaped by the choices students, educators, and institutions make in the next few years. The technology itself is neutral — it can make education better or worse, more equitable or less, more meaningful or more hollow.

The students who use AI to learn more deeply, think more critically, and produce more thoughtful work will push education in the right direction. The students who use AI to avoid learning will push it the wrong way — and ultimately hurt themselves most of all.

You get to choose which group you're in. This book has given you the tools, frameworks, and knowledge to make that choice well.

Choose wisely. The future is watching.

Part IX: Reference

"I am always doing that which I cannot do, in order that I may learn how to do it."

— Pablo Picasso

Epilogue: Your Toolkit, Your Responsibility

You've made it through the whole book. That tells me something about you: you're the kind of student who wants to do this right.

Let me leave you with something simple.

The tools in these pages are genuinely powerful. They can help you learn faster, research more effectively, write more clearly, study more efficiently, and prepare for a career where AI literacy is a baseline expectation. Used well, they make you a better student and a better thinker.

But they're tools. They don't learn for you. They don't think for you. They don't grow for you. The understanding you develop, the skills you build, the intellectual habits you form — those are yours. AI can't give them to you, and AI can't take them away once you have them.

The students I worry about aren't divided into the ones who use AI and the ones who don't. I worry about the ones who never figured out the difference between using AI to learn and using AI to avoid learning. That difference is small in the moment — a few extra minutes of effort, the discomfort of struggling with something before asking for help — but it compounds over four years into two very different graduates.

One has a degree and the skills it represents. The other has a degree and a gap where the skills should be.

You get to decide which one you are. Not once, but every day, with every assignment, in every moment when you choose between the shortcut and the process.

Reflecting on the Journey

Think back to where you were when you opened Chapter 1. Maybe AI felt like a mysterious black box. Maybe you were already using it but had a vague sense you were doing it wrong, or weren't getting everything you could out of it. Maybe you'd been told to avoid it entirely and felt like the world was moving on without you.

Now look at what you know. You understand how these tools work — not just at the surface level of typing and getting a response, but at the level that lets you use them deliberately. You know how to craft a prompt that gets what you actually need. You know how to use AI to study more effectively, break down complex concepts, prepare for exams, and strengthen your writing without letting it replace your voice. You know where the boundaries are — what AI does well, what it does poorly, and when to close the laptop and think for yourself.

That's not a small thing. Most people who use AI regularly have never thought about any of this with the care you just did. You've built a foundation that will serve you not just through the rest of your degree, but into whatever career follows it.

The Landscape Will Keep Changing

Let me be honest with you: parts of this book will be outdated within a year. Specific tools will evolve. New ones will appear. Features I described will be replaced by better ones. The AI landscape in 2028 will look different from the one I wrote about in 2026, just as 2026 looks nothing like 2024.

That's okay. What won't change is the framework you've built for thinking about these tools. The principles — use AI to deepen understanding, not to bypass it; verify what AI tells you; develop your own judgment alongside the AI's capabilities — those are durable. They'll apply to whatever tools come next, because they're not really about AI at all. They're about being a thoughtful, intentional learner in a world full of shortcuts.

When a new AI tool appears and your classmates scramble to figure out what it means for their workflow, you'll already have the mental model. You'll ask the right questions: What is this tool good at? Where does it fall short? How can I use it to learn more, not less? You'll adapt faster because you have a framework, not just instructions for a specific tool.

Keep Learning, Keep Questioning

The best students I've met share one trait: they stay curious even when they've been given the answer. AI will give you answers all day long. Your job is to keep asking whether those answers are right, whether they're complete, and whether you understand them well enough to explain them to someone else without the AI's help.

Don't stop experimenting. Try new tools when they come out. Push the boundaries of what you think AI can help you with — not to do less work, but to do different work, better work, work that challenges you in new ways. And when something doesn't work, when an AI gives you bad information or a prompt falls flat, treat that as data. You're learning what the tools can't do, which is just as valuable as learning what they can.

Talk to your professors about how you're using AI. Most of them aren't opposed to it — they're trying to figure it out too. The students who engage honestly about AI use, who show their work and explain their process, are the ones who build trust and earn the most latitude. Transparency isn't just an ethical choice. It's a strategic one.

The Process Is the Point

The struggle is the learning. AI makes the process more efficient, but it can't replace it.

Use these tools. Use them without guilt, without anxiety, without apology. But use them to become better — not just to produce better output.

Your education is one of the most valuable things you'll ever invest in. Protect it. Build on it. Make it real.

The world will need people who can think clearly, communicate effectively, and use powerful tools with integrity. After reading this book — and more importantly, after putting it into practice — you're well on your way to being one of those people.

You've got this.

Appendix A: Prompt Templates for Students

How to Use These Templates

Every template in this appendix follows the same principle from Chapter 4: use AI to understand, not to bypass. These are starting points, not magic formulas. The best prompts are specific to your actual assignment, your actual confusion, and your actual level of knowledge. Copy these, modify them, and make them yours.

A few rules for all of these templates:

- **Fill in the brackets.** Anything in [brackets] needs your specific information.
- **Be honest about what you don't understand.** The more specific you are about where you're stuck, the better the help you'll get.
- **Don't submit AI output as your own work.** These templates are designed to help you learn and produce better work — not to generate submissions.
- **Check your course policy first.** Some professors restrict AI use on certain assignments. When in doubt, ask.

Math

Concept Explanation

```
I'm studying [topic, e.g., "integration by parts"] in my [course level, e.g., "C
alculus II"] class.
I understand [what you do understand], but I'm confused about [specific confusio
n].
Can you explain [the concept] in plain language, then give me a simple example
and walk through it step by step?
```

Diagnosing a Wrong Answer

```
I'm working on this problem: [state the problem]
Here's my work:
Step 1: [your work]
Step 2: [your work]
Step 3: [your work]
I got [your answer] but the correct answer is [correct answer].

Find the exact step where I made an error. Tell me:
1. What kind of error it was (computational, conceptual, or notational)
2. Why I probably made it
3. How to avoid it next time
```

Practice Problem Generator

```
I need to practice [topic, e.g., "partial fraction decomposition"].
Generate 5 problems that increase in difficulty from straightforward to challeng
ing.
Don't solve them yet – just give me the problems. I'll attempt them and come bac
k
for feedback.
```

Proof Assistance

```
I need to prove that [statement to prove].
I know I should use [proof technique, e.g., "induction" or "contradiction"],
but I'm stuck on [specific part, e.g., "the inductive step"].
Don't write the proof for me. Instead:
1. Give me a hint about how to approach the part I'm stuck on
2. Remind me of the key definitions or theorems I'll need
3. Suggest what I should try first
```

Checking Your Own Work

```
I've completed this proof / solution: [paste your work]
Check it for:
1. Logical gaps – places where I skipped a step that needs justification
2. Errors in reasoning
3. Notation problems
Don't rewrite it. Just flag the issues so I can fix them myself.
```

Science

Understanding a Concept

```
I'm taking [course, e.g., "Organic Chemistry II"] and we're studying [topic].
My professor explained it as [how your professor described it], but I don't
understand [specific part].
Can you explain this in a different way? Use an analogy if it helps,
but make sure the analogy is scientifically accurate – don't oversimplify
in a way that would be wrong on an exam.
```

Lab Report Assistance

```
I'm writing a lab report for [experiment name/description].
My data shows [summarize your results].
I'm struggling with the [specific section: introduction/methods/results/discussi
on].

For the section I'm struggling with:
1. What should I include?
2. What's the logical structure?
3. What mistakes do students commonly make in this section?

Don't write the section for me – help me understand what it needs.
```

Data Analysis Support

```
I have the following dataset from my [course] lab: [describe or paste data]
I need to [what you need to do with it, e.g., "determine if there's a
statistically significant difference between groups"].
What statistical test should I use and why? Walk me through the logic
of choosing this test, not just the answer.
```

Connecting Theory to Experiment

```
In my [course] lab, we observed [what you observed].
According to our textbook, [what theory predicts should happen].
My observation [matches / doesn't match] the prediction.
Help me think through why. If there's a discrepancy, what are the most
likely explanations? Don't tell me which one is right – give me a framework
for figuring it out.
```

Exam Review — Science

```
I have an exam on [topic/chapter] in [course] in [timeframe].
The exam will cover: [list topics or chapters].
My weakest areas are: [be honest].

Create a study plan that:
1. Prioritizes my weak areas
2. Includes key concepts I must know
3. Lists common exam question types for these topics
4. Gives me 3 practice questions per weak area (don't solve them)
```

Humanities

Essay Thesis Development

```
I'm writing a [length] essay for my [course] class on [topic/prompt].
My initial thesis is: [your thesis].

Challenge my thesis:
1. What are the strongest counterarguments?
2. Where is my thesis vague or overly broad?
3. How could I make it more specific and arguable?
4. Suggest 2-3 alternative angles I might not have considered.

Don't rewrite my thesis. Help me strengthen it through critique.
```

Analyzing a Primary Source

```
I'm analyzing [text/artwork/document] for my [course] class.
Here's the passage / description: [paste or describe the source]

Help me develop my analysis:
1. What are the key rhetorical/literary/artistic choices the creator made?
2. What historical or cultural context is essential for understanding this?
3. What are common interpretations, and what are their limitations?
4. What questions should I be asking about this source that I'm not asking?
```

Comparing Theoretical Frameworks

```
I need to compare [Theory A] and [Theory B] for my [course] class.
I understand [Theory A] pretty well, but I'm struggling with [Theory B],
```

```
especially [specific aspect].

Explain [Theory B] in a way that highlights how it differs from [Theory A].
Then identify:
1. Where the two frameworks agree
2. Where they fundamentally conflict
3. What kinds of evidence would support each one
```

Historical Analysis Support

```
I'm writing about [historical event/period/figure] for my [course].
My argument is that [your argument].

Help me think through this:
1. What primary sources would strengthen my argument?
2. What are the major historiographic debates about this topic?
3. What context am I potentially overlooking?
4. Where might my argument be anachronistic (applying modern assumptions
   to a past context)?
```

Philosophy — Argument Construction

```
I'm constructing an argument about [philosophical topic] for my [course].
My position is: [your position].
The strongest objection I can think of is: [your anticipated objection].

Help me:
1. Formalize my argument into clear premises and a conclusion
2. Identify any hidden assumptions in my premises
3. Evaluate whether my anticipated objection is really the strongest one
4. Suggest how I might respond to the strongest objection
```

Writing

Brainstorming and Outlining

```
I need to write a [type of paper] on [topic] for my [course].
The assignment requirements are: [paste or summarize the prompt].
My initial ideas are: [your rough thoughts].

Help me organize my thinking:
1. What are the possible angles for this paper?
2. What's the most logical structure given my argument?
```

3. What evidence or examples would I need for each section?
4. What am I likely to forget to include?

Feedback on a Draft

Here's a draft of my [type of paper] for [course]: [paste your draft]

Give me feedback on:
1. Argument clarity – is my thesis clear and do my paragraphs support it?
2. Logical flow – are there gaps between sections or ideas?
3. Evidence use – am I supporting claims adequately?
4. Weak spots – which paragraph is the weakest and why?

Be specific. Don't rewrite anything – tell me what needs work and why.

Strengthening Transitions

I've written these two paragraphs back to back, but the transition feels rough: [paste both paragraphs]

What's the logical relationship between these paragraphs? What transitional strategy would connect them? Give me 2-3 options for how to bridge them – describe the approach, don't write the sentences for me.

Revising for Clarity

Here's a paragraph from my paper that my professor said is unclear: [paste the paragraph]

Help me understand what makes it unclear:
1. Are there sentences that try to do too much?
2. Is the paragraph's main point obvious, or buried?
3. Are there vague words I should replace with specific ones?
4. Suggest a clearer structure for the same ideas.

Citation Integration

I want to integrate this source into my paper:
Source: [title, author, key finding or quote]
My argument in this section is: [what you're arguing]

Help me think through:
1. Should I quote, paraphrase, or summarize this source here?
2. How does this source support (or complicate) my argument?

```
3. What's the best place in my paragraph to introduce this source?
4. How should I frame it – agree, disagree, extend, qualify?
```

Reverse Outline (Diagnosing a Messy Draft)

```
My paper feels disorganized but I can't figure out why.
Here's the full draft: [paste draft]

Create a reverse outline: for each paragraph, write one sentence
stating what that paragraph actually does. Then tell me:
1. Are any paragraphs doing the same thing?
2. Are any paragraphs off-topic?
3. What's the logical order, and does my current order match it?
4. Where are the gaps – what's missing?
```

Research

Understanding a Journal Article

```
I'm reading this article for my [course/research project]:
Title: [title]
Authors: [authors]
Abstract: [paste abstract]

I need to understand this paper but I'm struggling with
[specific section, e.g., "the methodology" or "the statistical analysis"].
Explain [the confusing part] in plain language. Don't oversimplify –
I'm a [year, e.g., "third-year"] student in [field], so I have some
background but not expertise.
```

Literature Review Organization

```
I'm conducting a literature review on [topic] for my [course/thesis].
Here are the sources I've found so far: [list sources with brief descriptions]

Help me organize these:
1. What themes or categories do these sources fall into?
2. Where do the sources agree and disagree?
3. What gaps do I see in my collection – what perspectives am I missing?
4. Suggest a logical structure for presenting this literature.
```

Developing Research Questions

```
I'm interested in researching [broad topic] for my [course/thesis/capstone].
I know I need to narrow this down.
My initial interest is in [what specifically interests you about the topic].
My constraints are: [length, timeline, resources available]

Help me develop this into a feasible research question:
1. What are 3-5 specific, answerable questions within this topic?
2. For each, what methodology would be appropriate?
3. Which ones are feasible given my constraints?
4. Which ones would make the strongest contribution to the field?
```

Source Evaluation

```
I found this source and I'm not sure if it's appropriate for my
academic paper:
[Title, author, publication, date, brief description]

Help me evaluate:
1. Is this a peer-reviewed, scholarly source?
2. What's the credibility of the publication venue?
3. Is it current enough for my topic?
4. What biases or limitations should I be aware of?
5. How would my professor likely view this as a source?
```

Synthesizing Multiple Sources

```
I need to synthesize these sources for my literature review.
They all address [topic] but from different angles:

Source 1: [brief summary]
Source 2: [brief summary]
Source 3: [brief summary]

Help me find the connections:
1. What's the common thread?
2. Where do they contradict each other?
3. How does each one build on or challenge the others?
4. What argument can I make by bringing them together?
```

Study Skills

Creating a Study Plan

```
I have [exam/finals] in [timeframe].
My courses are: [list courses and exam dates]
My strongest subjects are: [list]
My weakest subjects are: [list]
I have approximately [hours] available to study per day.

Create a day-by-day study schedule that:
1. Prioritizes weak subjects but doesn't neglect strong ones
2. Uses spaced repetition (revisits topics on multiple days)
3. Includes specific study techniques for each subject
4. Builds in breaks (I burn out after about [time] of continuous study)
```

Flashcard Generation

```
I need to memorize [type of content, e.g., "key terms for my biology exam"].
The topics are: [list topics]

Generate flashcards with:
- Front: a clear, specific question or prompt
- Back: a concise, accurate answer
Make them test understanding, not just recall. Include some cards that
require me to apply concepts, not just define them.
Generate [number] cards, starting with the most essential concepts.
```

Explaining It Back (Feynman Technique)

```
I think I understand [concept] but I'm not sure. Let me try to explain
it to you, and tell me where I'm wrong or incomplete:

[Your explanation of the concept]

Score my explanation:
1. What did I get right?
2. What did I get wrong or describe inaccurately?
3. What did I leave out that's important?
4. What would I need to add to get full marks on an exam question?
```

Practice Exam Generator

```
I have an exam on [topics] in my [course].
The exam format is: [multiple choice / short answer / essay / problem-solving /
mixed]
My professor tends to ask questions that [describe the style if you know it].

Generate a practice exam with [number] questions that:
1. Cover all the major topics
2. Match the format of my actual exam
3. Include a mix of difficulty levels
4. Focus especially on [your weak areas]

Don't provide answers yet – I'll take the exam first and then ask for feedback.
```

Weekly Review

```
This week in [course], we covered:
[List topics, readings, or lecture summaries from the week]

Help me consolidate what I learned:
1. What are the 3-5 most important takeaways from this week?
2. How does this week's material connect to previous weeks?
3. What should I make sure I understand before next week?
4. Generate 3 questions I should be able to answer if I understood everything.
```

Languages

Grammar Explanation

```
I'm learning [language] at [level, e.g., "intermediate / B1"].
I'm confused about [specific grammar point, e.g., "when to use the
subjunctive vs. indicative in Spanish"].

Explain this grammar rule:
1. When do I use it?
2. Give me 3 clear examples with English translations
3. What are the common mistakes learners make with this rule?
4. Give me 3 practice sentences to try (don't translate them – I'll try first)
```

Vocabulary in Context

```
I'm learning these vocabulary words in [language]: [list words]

For each word:
1. Give me the definition
2. Use it in a natural sentence (with translation)
3. Tell me one common collocation or phrase it appears in
4. Note any false friends or common confusion points for English speakers
```

Conversation Practice Setup

```
Let's practice [language] conversation. My level is [level].

Rules for this practice:
- Speak to me only in [language]
- If I make a grammar or vocabulary error, continue the conversation
  naturally but use the correct form in your response (implicit correction)
- Keep your vocabulary at my level, but include 1-2 new words per response
- After every 5 exchanges, give me a brief English summary of my errors

Let's start. [Topic: e.g., "ordering food at a restaurant" / "discussing
weekend plans" / "debating a current event"]
```

Writing Correction

```
I wrote this paragraph in [language] for my class: [paste your writing]

Correct my writing, but do it in layers:
1. First, list only the grammar errors (with corrections)
2. Then, list vocabulary choices that are technically correct but
   unnatural – what would a native speaker say instead?
3. Finally, rate my writing on a scale of A1-C2 and tell me what
   I'd need to improve to reach the next level.
```

Reading Comprehension Support

```
I'm reading this text in [language] for my class: [paste text or describe it]

I understand the general idea but I'm struggling with:
[Specific sentences, phrases, or sections]

For each part I'm struggling with:
1. Break down the grammar structure
2. Identify any idiomatic expressions
```

```
3. Provide a natural English translation
4. Explain why it's constructed that way (so I learn the pattern)
```

Listening and Pronunciation Guide

```
I'm working on pronunciation in [language].
I struggle with these sounds/words: [list specific sounds or words]

For each one:
1. Describe how to physically produce the sound (tongue position,
   airflow, etc.)
2. Give me minimal pairs (words that differ by only that sound)
3. Suggest a practice technique
4. Tell me which English sound is closest and how the target sound differs
```

Quick-Reference Templates

These are shorter templates for common, everyday academic situations:

"Explain Like I'm a Student"

```
Explain [concept] as if I'm a [year] student in [major] who has taken
[relevant prerequisite courses] but has never encountered this concept before.
```

"What Am I Missing?"

```
I'm working on [assignment] and my current approach is [describe your approach].
I feel like something is off but I can't identify what. What am I overlooking?
```

"Prepare Me for Office Hours"

```
I'm going to my professor's office hours to ask about [topic/problem].
Help me prepare:
1. What specific questions should I ask?
2. What should I review beforehand so I don't waste their time?
3. What should I bring (notes, attempts, specific examples)?
```

"Summarize This Reading"

```
I need to read [title/chapter] by [author] for [course] by [date].
The reading is about [brief description or paste abstract/introduction].
Give me a framework for what to pay attention to while reading —
```

```
key themes, arguments, terms — so I read actively instead of passively.
Don't summarize it for me. Tell me what to look for.
```

"Pre-Lecture Prep"

```
Tomorrow's lecture in [course] is on [topic].
Last week we covered [previous topic].
Give me a 5-minute briefing on what I should know going in:
1. Key terms I should recognize
2. How this connects to what we've already learned
3. One question I should be able to answer by the end of the lecture
```

"Why Does This Matter?"

```
I'm studying [topic] in [course] and I'm struggling to see why it matters.
Without being condescending, help me understand:
1. Why is this topic important in [field]?
2. What real-world problems does it solve?
3. What would I not be able to do if I didn't understand this?
```

A Final Note on Templates

The best prompt you'll ever write is one that honestly describes what you know, what you don't know, and what you need. No template can replace that honesty. Use these as scaffolding while you're learning to communicate effectively with AI, and eventually you'll outgrow them — which is exactly the point.

Appendix B: How to Cite AI-Assisted Work

Why This Matters

Citing AI use isn't just about following rules — it's about intellectual honesty. When you cite a book, you're saying "this idea came from here." When you cite AI, you're saying "this tool contributed to my process in this way." Your professor, your reader, and your future self all benefit from that transparency.

The major citation styles have all issued AI guidance. This appendix gives you the specific formats, with examples you can copy and adapt.

One important distinction before we start: how you cite AI depends on *how you used it*. Using AI to generate text differs from using AI to help you research, which differs from using AI to edit your writing. The citation should reflect what actually happened.

APA 7th Edition

The American Psychological Association updated its guidelines to address AI-generated content. Here's what you need to know.

AI-Generated Text

When AI produced text that you included (with modification or direct quotation) in your work:

Reference list entry:

> OpenAI. (2026). ChatGPT (March 2026 version) [Large language model]. https://chat.openai.com
>
> Anthropic. (2026). Claude (March 2026 version) [Large language model]. https://claude.ai

Google. (2026). Gemini (March 2026 version) [Large language model]. https://gemini.google.com

In-text citation:

> When prompted to explain the implications of quantum decoherence for biological systems, ChatGPT generated the following summary (OpenAI, 2026):

Format breakdown:

Element	What to write
Author	The company (OpenAI, Anthropic, Google, etc.)
Date	Year of the version you used
Title	Name of the AI tool, with version in parentheses
Description	[Large language model] in brackets
URL	Link to the tool

Key rules: - The AI company is the author, not "ChatGPT" itself. - Include the version or date of the model you used. - Describe the nature of the prompt in your text — the reader should understand what you asked. - Since chat conversations aren't retrievable by readers, APA treats AI output similarly to personal communications in some contexts. When you're using AI output as a source, though, a reference list entry is appropriate.

AI-Assisted Research

When you used AI as a research tool (finding sources, summarizing literature, generating search terms) but the writing is entirely yours:

In-text acknowledgment (no reference entry needed):

> Initial search terms for this literature review were developed with the assistance of Claude (Anthropic, 2026), an AI language model. All sources were independently verified and evaluated by the author.

When to use this approach: When AI helped you *find* or *understand* things but didn't contribute text to your paper. Similar to acknowledging a database or research assistant.

AI-Edited Work

When you used AI to revise, proofread, or improve your own writing:

In-text or methodology acknowledgment:

> Drafts of this paper were reviewed using Gemini (Google, 2026) for grammar, clarity, and structural suggestions. All revisions were made by the author.

Key point: If AI suggested edits and you accepted them, that's your editorial choice — you don't need to cite each suggestion. But disclosing that AI was part of your revision process is good practice and increasingly expected.

APA Formatting Template

Copy and adapt:

```
[Company]. ([Year]). [AI Tool Name] ([Version/Date]) [Large language model].
    [URL]
```

MLA 9th Edition

The Modern Language Association treats AI-generated text as a work with an author (the AI company) and a tool (the AI system).

AI-Generated Text

Works Cited entry:

> "Describe the symbolism of the green light in The Great Gatsby" prompt. ChatGPT, version GPT-4o, OpenAI, 15 Mar. 2026, chat.openai.com.
>
> "Explain the difference between structuralism and post-structuralism" prompt. Claude, version Claude Opus, Anthropic, 22 Mar. 2026, claude.ai.

In-text citation:

> ChatGPT characterized the green light as "a layered symbol operating simultaneously as personal aspiration, class critique, and temporal impossibility" ("Describe the symbolism").

Format breakdown:

Element	What to write
Title of source	The prompt you used, in quotation marks, followed by "prompt"
Title of container	Name of the AI tool
Version	Model version
Publisher	The company
Date	Date you generated the output
Location	URL of the tool

Key rules: - MLA treats the prompt as the title of the source. - Include the specific date you generated the response (AI outputs aren't stable — the same prompt may produce different results on different days). - Keep the prompt text reasonably concise in the citation. If your prompt was very long, use a shortened version.

AI-Assisted Research

Works Cited entry is generally not needed. Instead, acknowledge AI use in your paper's methodology or a note:

> Research for this paper was aided by Perplexity AI, which was used to identify initial sources and generate search queries. All sources were independently located and evaluated.

AI-Edited Work

Acknowledgment in a note or methodology section:

> Drafts of this paper were reviewed for clarity and grammar using Claude (Anthropic). All editorial decisions were made by the author.

MLA Formatting Template

Copy and adapt:

```
"[Your prompt, shortened if necessary]" prompt. [AI Tool], version [version],
    [Company], [Day Month Year], [URL].
```

Chicago/Turabian 17th Edition

Chicago offers two systems: notes-bibliography (humanities) and author-date (sciences and social sciences). Here are both.

Notes-Bibliography System

For AI-Generated Text:

Footnote/endnote:

1. ChatGPT, response to "Analyze the economic factors that led to the 2008 financial crisis," OpenAI, March 15, 2026, https://chat.openai.com.
2. Claude, response to "Compare Kantian ethics with utilitarian ethics on the question of lying," Anthropic, March 22, 2026, https://claude.ai.

Bibliography entry:

ChatGPT. Response to "Analyze the economic factors that led to the 2008 financial crisis." OpenAI. March 15, 2026. https://chat.openai.com.

Shortened footnote (for subsequent citations):

3. ChatGPT, response to "Analyze the economic factors."

Author-Date System

For AI-Generated Text:

Reference list entry:

OpenAI. 2026. ChatGPT, response to "Explain the prisoner's dilemma in game theory." March 15, 2026. https://chat.openai.com.

In-text citation:

(OpenAI 2026)

AI-Assisted Research (Both Systems)

Include a note or acknowledgment:

> Research for this paper was supported by AI tools. Claude (Anthropic) was used to summarize and compare secondary sources identified through the university library database. All analysis and conclusions are the author's own.

AI-Edited Work (Both Systems)

Footnote or acknowledgment:

> Portions of this paper were reviewed for style and grammar using an AI writing assistant (Gemini, Google). All substantive content and editorial decisions are the author's.

Chicago Formatting Templates

Notes-bibliography footnote:

```
[AI Tool], response to "[prompt]," [Company], [Month Day, Year], [URL].
```

Notes-bibliography entry:

```
[AI Tool]. Response to "[prompt]." [Company]. [Month Day, Year]. [URL].
```

Author-date reference:

```
[Company]. [Year]. [AI Tool], response to "[prompt]." [Month Day, Year]. [URL].
```

IEEE Format

The Institute of Electrical and Electronics Engineers (IEEE) citation style is standard in engineering, computer science, and many technical fields. IEEE uses numbered references in the order they appear in the text.

AI-Generated Text

Reference list entry:

[1] OpenAI, "ChatGPT response to 'Explain the trade-offs between TCP and UDP for real-time applications,'" Mar. 15, 2026. [Online]. Available: https://chat.openai.com

[2] Anthropic, "Claude response to 'Describe the advantages of transformer architectures over RNNs,'" Mar. 22, 2026. [Online]. Available: https://claude.ai

In-text citation:

The AI assistant described the trade-offs in terms of latency, reliability, and overhead [1].

Format breakdown:

Element	What to write
Author	The company (OpenAI, Anthropic, Google, etc.)
Title	Description of the AI response and your prompt, in quotation marks
Date	Month and year you generated the output
Medium	[Online]
URL	Available: followed by the tool's URL

Key rules: - IEEE numbers references in the order they first appear in the text. Reuse the same number if you cite the same AI interaction again. - Include enough of the prompt in the title field for the reader to understand what was asked. - Since AI outputs aren't permanently retrievable, treat these like personal communications when your instructor requires it.

AI-Assisted Research

In-text acknowledgment (no numbered reference needed):

AI tools were used during the literature survey phase of this work. Perplexity AI was used to identify relevant papers, and all sources were independently verified by the author.

Where to place it: IEEE papers usually put this in an acknowledgment section at the end, before references.

AI-Edited Work

Acknowledgment section:

> The authors used Gemini (Google) to review drafts for grammar and technical clarity. All technical content and editorial decisions are the authors' own.

IEEE Formatting Template

Copy and adapt:

```
[#] Company, "AI Tool response to 'your prompt,'" Month Day, Year.
    [Online]. Available: URL
```

ACS Format

The American Chemical Society (ACS) citation style is used in chemistry and related scicnces. ACS supports multiple formats (superscript numbers, italic numbers, or author-date); the numbered format is most common and shown here.

AI-Generated Text

Reference list entry:

(1) OpenAI. ChatGPT Response to "Explain the Difference Between SN1 and SN2 Reaction Mechanisms." https://chat.openai.com (accessed 2026-03-15).
(2) Anthropic. Claude Response to "Describe the Role of Catalysts in Haber-Bosch Process Optimization." https://claude.ai (accessed 2026-03-22).

In-text citation (superscript style):

> The AI model described the mechanistic differences in terms of substrate geometry and nucleophile strength.[1]

Format breakdown:

Element	What to write

Element	What to write
Number	Numbered in order of appearance
Author	The company
Title	Description of the AI response and prompt, in title case
URL	The tool's URL
Access date	Date you generated the response, in parentheses

Key rules: - ACS treats AI output similarly to web-based resources — include the access date because the content isn't stable. - Use title case for the description of the response. - If your instructor prefers author-date format, use (OpenAI, 2026) in the text.

AI-Assisted Research

Acknowledgment (typically in the Acknowledgments section):

> Literature searches were supported by Perplexity AI and Semantic Scholar. All cited sources were independently retrieved and evaluated by the authors.

AI-Edited Work

Acknowledgment section:

> Drafts of this manuscript were reviewed for grammar and clarity using Claude (Anthropic). All scientific content and editorial decisions are the authors' own.

ACS Formatting Template

Copy and adapt:

```
(#) Company. AI Tool Response to "Your Prompt." URL (accessed YYYY-MM-DD).
```

What to Do When You're Unsure

If your citation style hasn't explicitly addressed AI, or your professor has specific requirements, follow this decision tree:

1. **Check your assignment instructions.** Some professors specify exactly how they want AI use disclosed.
2. **Check your style guide's latest edition or website.** APA, MLA, and Chicago all update their guidance online more often than they publish new editions.
3. **Check your school's AI policy.** Some institutions have standardized disclosure requirements that override style guide conventions.
4. **When in doubt, over-disclose.** Saying more about how you used AI is always safer than saying less. No professor will penalize you for being too transparent.
5. **Ask your professor.** If you're genuinely unsure, a quick email asking "how would you like me to cite my AI use on this assignment?" shows integrity and conscientiousness.

Common Mistakes to Avoid

Citing AI as if it were a human author. AI has no expertise, credentials, or scholarly reputation. Don't treat a ChatGPT response as equivalent to a peer-reviewed source. If AI helped you find a source, cite the actual source — not the AI.

Failing to specify how you used AI. "I used ChatGPT" tells your professor nothing. "I used ChatGPT to generate an initial outline, then wrote the paper myself, reorganizing and expanding on the AI's structural suggestions" tells them everything they need to know.

Assuming one citation covers all AI use. If you used AI at multiple stages — brainstorming, drafting, editing, research — each stage warrants its own acknowledgment.

Citing the AI but not the actual sources. If AI pointed you toward a journal article and you read and used that article, cite the article. AI was the discovery mechanism, not the source. You don't cite Google Scholar when you use it to find a paper; the same principle applies to AI.

Sample Disclosure Statement

Many professors now ask for a disclosure statement describing your AI use. Here's a template you can adapt:

```
AI Use Disclosure

In completing this assignment, I used [AI tool(s)] in the following ways:

1. [Describe first use, e.g., "I used Claude to brainstorm thesis
   statement options. I chose one and modified it."]
2. [Describe second use, e.g., "I used ChatGPT to explain a concept
   from the assigned reading that I didn't understand after my
   first reading."]
3. [Describe third use, e.g., "I used Grammarly's AI features to
   check my final draft for grammar and clarity."]

All submitted text is my own writing. [OR: Sections X and Y incorporate
AI-generated text that I have modified and cited in the paper.]
```

Adapt this to your situation. Be specific, be honest, keep it brief. Your professor doesn't need a novel — they need to know what you did and how.

Appendix C: Understanding Your School's AI Policy

Why You Need to Read the Policy

Here's a truth most students don't want to hear: "I didn't know" is not a defense against an academic integrity violation. Every university's academic integrity policy includes some version of "students are responsible for understanding and following these policies." That includes AI policies.

The good news: most AI policies aren't complicated. They just need to be read carefully, because the details matter. A policy that says "AI may be used for brainstorming but not for drafting" draws a very specific line. Skip the read and you'll cross that line by accident. Read it and you can use AI confidently within the boundaries.

This appendix gives you the tools to find, read, and understand your school's AI policy — and to handle the (still common) situation where no clear policy exists.

How to Find Your School's AI Policy

AI policies live in different places depending on the institution. Check these locations in order:

1. **Your course syllabus.** The most important document. Many professors include AI-specific sections in their syllabi. If the syllabus addresses AI, that's your binding policy for that course — even if it differs from the university-wide policy.
2. **Your university's academic integrity page.** Most universities have updated their academic integrity policies to address AI. Look for the Dean of Students office, the Provost's page, or the Academic Integrity office website.

3. **Your department's website.** Some departments (especially English, Computer Science, and Engineering) have issued department-level guidance more specific than the university-wide policy.

4. **Your university's teaching and learning center.** Many schools publish AI guidance for faculty that's also available to students. These documents often offer the most detailed and nuanced guidance.

5. **Your LMS (Canvas, Blackboard, Moodle).** Some professors post AI policies on the course page rather than in the syllabus.

If you can't find a policy: that doesn't mean anything goes. See the section below on what to do when no policy exists.

How to Read an AI Policy

AI policies use specific language that means specific things. Here's a decoder:

Restrictive Language

What the policy says	What it means
"AI tools may not be used on any assignment"	Total ban. Don't use AI for anything you submit.
"Work must be entirely your own"	Ambiguous, but likely means no AI-generated text. Ask for clarification.
"AI-generated content constitutes academic dishonesty"	AI-generated text in your submission = integrity violation.
"Students must demonstrate independent mastery"	Likely means proctored or in-class assessment; AI may be restricted.

Permissive Language

What the policy says	What it means
"AI may be used as a learning aid"	You can use AI to understand things, but not to produce submissions.
"AI-assisted work is permitted with disclosure"	You can use AI in your process, but you must say how.

What the policy says	What it means
"Students are encouraged to explore AI tools"	Professor is pro-AI. Still read the specific assignment instructions.
"AI use is permitted for [specific tasks]"	Only those specific tasks. Everything else is off-limits.

The Dangerous Middle

What the policy says	What it means
"Use your judgment"	The professor hasn't thought this through. Err on the side of caution and disclose everything.
"AI policy varies by assignment"	Read every single assignment's instructions carefully.
No mention of AI at all	See the next section.

Red Flags

Watch out for policies that: - **Rely on AI detection tools as the sole method of enforcement.** Detection tools have high false-positive rates. If your school uses detection software and you're flagged incorrectly, know your appeal rights. - **Are vague about consequences.** A good policy specifies what happens for a first offense vs. a repeated offense. - **Don't distinguish between types of AI use.** Using AI to brainstorm and using AI to write your paper are fundamentally different acts. A policy that treats them identically is poorly designed.

What to Do When No Policy Exists

It's 2026 and some courses, departments, and even institutions still don't have explicit AI policies. Here's how to handle it:

Step 1: Default to Conservative Use

Until you have explicit permission, assume that AI-generated text submitted as your own work isn't allowed. This is a safe default because: - Traditional academic integrity policies already prohibit submitting work that isn't yours. - AI-generated text isn't your work, even if you prompted it. - "The policy didn't mention AI" has never successfully defended a student in an integrity hearing when the underlying act was clearly not the student's own work.

Step 2: Email Your Professor

Here's a template you can adapt:

```
Subject: Question about AI tool use in [Course Name]

Dear Professor [Name],

I want to make sure I understand the expectations for AI tool use in
[Course Name/Number]. I've reviewed the syllabus and the university's
academic integrity policy, and I want to clarify what is and isn't
appropriate.

Specifically, I'd like to know:
1. Is it acceptable to use AI tools (like ChatGPT or Claude) to help
   me understand course concepts?
2. Are there assignments where AI use is permitted, restricted, or
   prohibited?
3. If AI use is permitted, how would you like me to disclose it?

I want to use these tools responsibly and within your expectations.
Thank you for the clarification.

Best regards,
[Your name]
[Course and section number]
```

Most professors will appreciate this email. It shows conscientiousness and gives them a chance to articulate expectations they may not have formalized.

Step 3: Save the Response

Whatever your professor says, save it. Screenshot the email. If there's ever a question about your AI use later, you'll want documentation that you asked and got specific guidance.

Questions to Ask Your Professor

Beyond the email template above, here are specific questions for specific situations:

Before the Semester Starts

- "Will AI policies be consistent across all assignments, or will they vary?"
- "Is there a preferred AI disclosure format you'd like us to use?"
- "Are there specific AI tools you recommend or prohibit?"

Before a Specific Assignment

- "Can I use AI to brainstorm ideas for this paper, or do you want the ideation to be entirely my own?"
- "Is it okay to use AI to check my grammar and style after I've written my draft?"
- "If I use AI to understand a concept from the readings, do I need to disclose that?"

If You've Been Flagged by AI Detection

- "Can you tell me which detection tool was used and what confidence level it reported?"
- "I wrote this work myself. Can I meet with you to discuss the content and demonstrate my understanding?"
- "What is the appeal process if I believe the detection result is a false positive?"
- "Can I show you my drafts, notes, or revision history as evidence of my writing process?"

If the Policy Seems Unfair or Unclear

- "I want to follow the policy, but I'm not sure how [specific scenario] fits within it. Can you clarify?"
- "The university policy and your syllabus seem to differ on [point]. Which one should I follow for this course?"
- "I notice the policy doesn't address [scenario]. What's your expectation?"

Sample AI Usage Policies

These model policies represent the common approaches you'll encounter. They aren't real policies from specific institutions, but they reflect the patterns in actual policies as of 2026.

Model Policy A: Restrictive

> **AI Use Policy**
>
> The use of artificial intelligence tools, including but not limited to ChatGPT, Claude, Gemini, and Copilot, is prohibited on all graded assignments in this course. This includes using AI to generate text, solve problems, produce code, create outlines, or draft any portion of submitted work.
>
> Students may use AI tools for general learning purposes (e.g., asking an AI to explain a concept covered in lecture), but no AI-generated content may appear in any submitted work.
>
> Use of AI on graded work will be treated as a violation of the Academic Integrity Code and referred to the Dean of Students.
>
> **What this means for you:** You can use AI to study and learn, but your submitted work must be 100% yours. Keep your learning conversations with AI separate from your assignments.

Model Policy B: Moderate / Disclosure Required

> **AI Use Policy**
>
> Students may use AI tools as part of their academic workflow, provided that:
>
> 1. All AI use is disclosed in an AI Use Statement submitted with the assignment.
> 2. AI-generated text is not submitted verbatim. Students must substantially transform any AI output incorporated into their work.
> 3. Students can demonstrate understanding of all submitted content if asked.
> 4. AI use does not replace the core learning objectives of the assignment.
>
> Specific assignments may have additional restrictions, which will be noted in the assignment instructions.

Failure to disclose AI use, or submission of substantially AI-generated work without transformation, constitutes a violation of the Academic Integrity Code.

What this means for you: You can use AI, but you must say how, and the work must still fundamentally be yours. Think of AI as a tool in your process, not a ghostwriter.

Model Policy C: Permissive / AI-Encouraged

AI Use Policy

This course encourages the thoughtful use of AI tools as part of the learning process. AI literacy is a core skill, and learning to work effectively with AI is one of the course objectives.

Students are expected to:

1. Use AI critically — verify AI-generated information, identify errors, and refine AI outputs.
2. Document their AI use in a process reflection submitted with each assignment.
3. Demonstrate understanding of all submitted content during in-class discussions and examinations.

Assignments will specify whether AI use is required, encouraged, optional, or restricted. When not specified, students may use AI with appropriate documentation.

What this means for you: This professor wants you to use AI — but thoughtfully and transparently. The focus is on your process, not just your product. Document what you did and be prepared to discuss it.

Model Policy D: Assignment-Specific

AI Use Policy

AI tool permissions vary by assignment in this course:

- **Research papers:** AI may be used for brainstorming, outlining, and finding sources. AI may not be used to generate draft text. Disclosure required.
- **Problem sets:** AI may not be used. Problems must be solved independently or with approved study partners.

- **Lab reports:** AI may be used to check grammar and clarity of your written draft. AI may not be used to generate analysis or conclusions. Disclosure required.
- **Final project:** AI use is unrestricted, but a comprehensive AI Use Statement is required describing all tools used and how they contributed to the project.

Each assignment will include an AI permissions indicator: [No AI], [Limited AI], or [Open AI].

What this means for you: Read every assignment carefully. The rules change depending on what you're working on.

When No Policy Exists: A Student-Proposed Template

Sometimes there's no policy at all — not in the syllabus, not on the department website, nowhere. In that situation, take the initiative by proposing a simple AI usage agreement to your professor or department. This shows leadership and good faith, and it gives your professor something concrete to respond to.

Here's a template you can adapt and send as an email attachment, a shared document, or a printed handout:

```
Proposed AI Usage Guidelines for [Course Name / Department]

Prepared by: [Your name, date]

Purpose: To establish clear, shared expectations for the use of AI
tools in coursework, in the absence of an existing policy.

1. PERMITTED USES
   - Using AI to explain concepts covered in class
   - Using AI to brainstorm ideas or generate outlines
   - Using AI to check grammar and clarity on completed drafts
   - Using AI to find and summarize potential sources (with
     independent verification)

2. RESTRICTED USES (require explicit instructor permission)
   - Using AI to generate draft text for submission
   - Using AI to solve assigned problems
   - Using AI to produce code for graded assignments
```

```
3. PROHIBITED USES
   - Submitting AI-generated work as one's own without disclosure
   - Using AI during proctored exams unless explicitly allowed
   - Sharing AI outputs in ways that facilitate academic dishonesty

4. DISCLOSURE REQUIREMENT
   Students will include a brief AI Use Statement with any assignment
   where AI tools were used, describing which tools were used and how.

5. GOOD FAITH CLAUSE
   These guidelines are proposed in good faith and are open to
   revision based on instructor feedback. The goal is clarity and
   transparency, not to expand or restrict AI use beyond what the
   instructor considers appropriate.
```

A few tips for proposing this:

- **Frame it as a question, not a demand.** Try: "I drafted this as a starting point — would something like this work for our class?"
- **Offer it as a convenience.** Professors are busy. Reacting to a draft is easier than writing one from scratch.
- **Be ready to accept changes.** Your professor may cross out half of it or rewrite it entirely. Fine — the goal was to start the conversation.
- **Share it early in the semester.** Most useful in the first few weeks, before anyone runs into trouble.

If your professor adopts something like this — even informally — everyone in the class benefits from clearer expectations.

Your Rights

You have rights in the academic integrity process. Know these:

1. **Right to clear expectations.** You're entitled to know the rules before you can be held accountable for breaking them. If a policy is genuinely ambiguous, the ambiguity should be resolved in your favor.

2. **Right to due process.** Every accredited institution has an appeal process for academic integrity cases. If you're accused of an AI-related

violation, you have the right to present your side, provide evidence, and appeal the decision.

3. **Right to challenge detection tools.** AI detection software isn't infallible. If you're flagged and you didn't use AI, you have the right to challenge the finding. Request to know which tool was used, its confidence level, and what evidence supports the accusation beyond the software's output.

4. **Right to consistent enforcement.** A policy enforced against some students but not others isn't a legitimate policy. If you believe enforcement is inconsistent, document the inconsistency and raise it in your appeal.

5. **Right to ask questions.** Asking your professor about AI policies isn't suspicious behavior. It's responsible behavior. Never let fear of seeming suspicious prevent you from seeking clarity.

One Last Thing

Policies will keep changing. The AI landscape in 2026 already differs from 2024, and 2028 will differ from 2026. The best habit you can build isn't memorizing any specific policy — it's the habit of checking, asking, and disclosing. Do those three things consistently and you'll navigate whatever policy environment you encounter.

Appendix D: Glossary

This glossary defines AI terms you'll encounter in this book, in your courses, and in the broader conversation about AI in education. Definitions are written for students, not engineers — but they're accurate. If a term has a more precise technical meaning, it's noted.

AI (Artificial Intelligence) The broad field of computer science focused on building systems that can perform tasks typically requiring human intelligence — understanding language, recognizing patterns, making decisions, generating content. When people say "AI" in 2026, they usually mean generative AI (see below), but the field is much larger than that.

AI Detection Tool Software designed to determine whether text was written by a human or generated by AI. Examples include Turnitin's AI detection feature and GPTZero. These tools work by analyzing statistical patterns in writing, but they produce both false positives (flagging human-written text as AI) and false negatives (missing AI-generated text). No detection tool is reliable enough to serve as sole evidence of academic dishonesty.

AI Hallucination When an AI generates information that sounds confident and plausible but is factually incorrect. This includes fabricated citations, invented statistics, and made-up facts presented as real. Hallucinations happen because AI models generate text based on patterns, not knowledge — they predict what sounds right, not what is right. Always verify AI output against reliable sources.

AI Literacy The ability to understand what AI can and can't do, use AI tools effectively, evaluate AI output critically, and make informed decisions about when and how to use AI. This is increasingly considered a core competency alongside traditional literacy and numeracy.

Algorithm A set of rules or instructions that a computer follows to solve a problem or complete a task. AI systems rely on extremely complex algorithms — but at their core, they're still just sequences of steps.

API (Application Programming Interface) A way for software systems to communicate with each other. When an app "uses AI," it's usually connecting to an AI model through an API rather than running the AI itself. Relevant to students because many tools you use (Notion AI, Grammarly, research tools) access AI models through APIs.

Bias (in AI) Systematic errors in AI output that reflect biases present in the training data or the design of the system. For example, if an AI was trained mostly on English-language academic texts, it may underrepresent perspectives from non-English-speaking scholars. AI bias is particularly important to understand for research and analysis tasks.

Chatbot An AI system designed for conversation. ChatGPT, Claude, and Gemini are chatbots, though they're far more capable than the simple customer service chatbots that preceded them. The conversational interface makes them intuitive to use, but it can also make them feel more authoritative than they are.

Claude An AI assistant developed by Anthropic. Known for careful reasoning, nuanced responses, and strong performance on academic tasks. Available in free and paid tiers.

Context Window The maximum amount of text an AI can consider at once — including both your input and its output. Think of it as the AI's working memory. A larger context window means the AI can handle longer documents, remember more of your conversation, and work with more complex inputs. Context windows in 2026 range from roughly 100,000 to over 1,000,000 tokens.

Copilot (Microsoft) Microsoft's AI assistant, integrated across Microsoft 365 products (Word, Excel, PowerPoint, Outlook, etc.). Uses OpenAI's technology. Relevant to students because many schools provide Microsoft 365 access, which may include Copilot features.

Deep Learning A type of machine learning that uses neural networks with many layers (hence "deep") to learn complex patterns from data. Deep learning is the technical foundation behind modern AI capabilities like language understanding, image generation, and speech recognition.

Few-Shot Prompting A technique where you give the AI a few examples of what you want before asking it to generate something. For instance, showing the AI three example flashcards before asking it to generate more. This helps the AI understand the format and quality level you're expecting.

Fine-Tuning The process of taking a pre-trained AI model and training it further on a specific dataset to make it better at a particular task. Some academic tools use fine-tuned versions of large language models to provide specialized assistance in areas like scientific writing or legal research.

Foundation Model A large AI model trained on a broad dataset that can be adapted for many different tasks. GPT-5, Claude, and Gemini are all foundation models. They weren't trained specifically for education — they were trained broadly and then applied to educational use cases (among many others).

Generative AI AI that creates new content — text, images, code, music, video. This is the category of AI most relevant to students in 2026. ChatGPT, Claude, Gemini, Midjourney, and GitHub Copilot are all generative AI tools.

Gemini Google's AI assistant. Integrates with Google Workspace (Docs, Sheets, Gmail, etc.) and Google Search. Available in free and paid tiers.

GPT (Generative Pre-trained Transformer) The architecture behind OpenAI's models. "GPT-5.4" and its reasoning variants are specific versions. The name describes the technique: generative (creates content), pre-trained (learned from a massive dataset before deployment), transformer (the specific neural network architecture used). You'll sometimes see "GPT" used loosely to mean any large language model, but technically it refers to OpenAI's models.

Grounding The process of connecting AI output to verifiable sources. When an AI "grounds" its response, it ties its claims to specific, checkable references. Perplexity AI, for example, provides inline citations that ground its responses. Grounded responses are easier to verify and more trustworthy for academic work.

Guardrails Safety measures built into AI systems to prevent harmful, inappropriate, or unreliable outputs. Guardrails are why AI will refuse certain requests or add disclaimers to sensitive topics. They're imperfect — AI can sometimes be "jailbroken" past its guardrails — but they represent an important layer of responsible design.

Hallucination See *AI Hallucination*.

Large Language Model (LLM) The type of AI system that powers ChatGPT, Claude, Gemini, and similar tools. LLMs are trained on massive amounts of text data and learn to predict what comes next in a sequence of words. Despite the name, modern LLMs handle more than just language — they can process images, write code, and reason about complex problems. But "language model" remains the technical term.

Machine Learning A branch of AI where systems learn patterns from data rather than following explicitly programmed rules. Instead of telling a computer "if X, then Y," you give it thousands of examples and let it figure out the patterns itself. Machine learning is the broader category that includes deep learning and other techniques.

Model In the AI context, a "model" is the trained system that processes inputs and generates outputs. When someone says "the model hallucinated" or "this model is better at math," they're referring to the specific AI system doing the work. Different models have different strengths — some are better at creative writing, others at mathematical reasoning.

Multimodal An AI system that can process multiple types of input — text, images, audio, video — rather than just one. Most leading AI models in 2026 are multimodal: you can upload a photo of a handwritten equation, a screenshot of a graph, or a diagram from your textbook, and the AI can work with it.

Natural Language Processing (NLP) The branch of AI focused on enabling computers to understand, interpret, and generate human language. Every time you type a question to ChatGPT or Claude, NLP is what allows the system to understand what you're asking.

Neural Network A computing system loosely inspired by the structure of biological brains. It consists of layers of interconnected nodes (neurons) that process information. Neural networks are the foundation of modern AI — they're how AI models learn patterns from data.

NotebookLM Google's AI-powered research and note-taking tool. Particularly useful for students because it works directly with your uploaded documents and grounds its responses in your sources rather than its general training data.

Open Source (AI) AI models whose code and sometimes training data are publicly available for anyone to use, modify, and build on. Examples include Meta's Llama models and Mistral's models. Open-source AI matters for students because it means AI capabilities aren't locked behind a few companies' products.

Perplexity AI An AI-powered search and research tool that provides answers with inline citations to real sources. Particularly useful for academic research because it shows where its information comes from, making verification easier.

Prompt The text you type into an AI system — your question, instruction, or request. Prompt quality significantly affects output quality. A vague prompt produces a vague response; a specific prompt with context produces a useful response. The templates in Appendix A are designed to help you write better prompts.

Prompt Engineering The practice of crafting prompts to get the best possible output from an AI system. This includes techniques like providing context, specifying the format you want, giving examples, and assigning the AI a role. It's a learnable skill, not a mysterious art.

RAG (Retrieval-Augmented Generation) A technique where an AI retrieves relevant information from a specific database or document collection before generating its response. This reduces hallucinations because the AI is working from real sources rather than just its training data. NotebookLM and Perplexity both use RAG-like approaches.

System Prompt Instructions given to an AI model before your conversation that define how it should behave. When a professor sets up an AI tool for a class, they might use a system prompt like "You are a Socratic tutor. Never give direct answers. Always guide the student through questions." You don't always see the system prompt, but it shapes how the AI responds to you.

Temperature A setting that controls how random or creative an AI's responses are. Low temperature produces more predictable, focused responses. High temperature produces more varied, creative (but potentially less accurate) responses. For academic work, lower temperatures are generally better.

Token The basic unit of text that AI models process. A token is roughly three-quarters of a word in English. When AI tools reference context windows, token limits, or pricing, they're counting tokens. The concept matters to you primarily when working with long documents — if your paper exceeds the AI's token limit, it can't process the whole thing at once.

Training Data The massive dataset an AI model learned from. For large language models, this typically includes books, websites, scientific papers, code repositories, and other text sources. The training data determines what the AI "knows" — and also what biases it carries. Training data has a cutoff date, which means AI models may not know about very recent events.

Transformer The neural network architecture behind most modern AI language models. Introduced in a 2017 research paper titled "Attention Is All You Need," the transformer architecture enabled AI models to process language much more effectively than previous approaches. The "T" in GPT and the architecture behind Claude and Gemini are all transformers.

Zero-Shot Prompting Asking an AI to perform a task without providing any examples — just the instruction. This is how most people interact with AI: "Explain quantum entanglement in simple terms." Compare with *few-shot prompting*, where you provide examples first.

Appendix E: Resources

Free AI Tools for Students

You don't need to spend money to get meaningful value from AI. Every tool below has a free tier genuinely useful for academic work. Paid upgrades exist for all of them, but start here.

General-Purpose AI Assistants

ChatGPT (Free Tier) chat.openai.com OpenAI's flagship chatbot. The free tier provides access to GPT-5.4 with usage limits. Good for concept explanations, brainstorming, writing feedback, and problem-solving. Limitations: usage caps during peak hours, no access to the latest reasoning variants.

Claude (Free Tier) claude.ai Anthropic's AI assistant. Known for careful reasoning, strong performance on nuanced questions, and long context windows. The free tier is generous enough for most academic tasks. Particularly strong for essay feedback, complex analysis, and research synthesis.

Gemini (Free Tier) gemini.google.com Google's AI assistant. Integrates with Google Workspace, which many students already use. Good for research, summarization, and working with Google Docs. The free tier includes access to Gemini's core capabilities.

Microsoft Copilot (Free Tier) copilot.microsoft.com Microsoft's AI assistant. If your school provides Microsoft 365, you may have Copilot access included. Useful for working within Word, Excel, and PowerPoint. The free web version provides general-purpose AI chat.

Research Tools

Perplexity AI (Free Tier) perplexity.ai An AI-powered research tool that provides answers with inline citations. The free tier gives you a limited number of "Pro" searches per day, but standard searches are unlimited. Excellent for finding sources and getting answers you can verify.

Google Scholar scholar.google.com Not AI-powered in the chatbot sense, but essential for academic research. Free, comprehensive, and the standard starting point for finding peer-reviewed sources. Use it alongside AI tools, not instead of them.

Semantic Scholar semanticscholar.org An AI-powered academic search engine from the Allen Institute for AI. Provides AI-generated summaries of papers, citation context, and related work recommendations. Completely free. Particularly useful for literature reviews.

Connected Papers connectedpapers.com Builds visual graphs of related academic papers. Enter one paper, and it maps the network of related research. Free tier provides limited graphs per month. Excellent for discovering sources you wouldn't have found otherwise.

Elicit elicit.com An AI research assistant that helps you find papers, extract claims, and synthesize findings across sources. Free tier available. Designed specifically for academic research, which makes it more focused than general-purpose chatbots for this task.

Writing Tools

Grammarly (Free Tier) grammarly.com Grammar, spelling, and clarity checking with AI-powered suggestions. The free tier covers the basics. The paid tier adds more advanced style and tone features, but the free version is solid for proofreading. Many schools provide Grammarly Premium for students — check with your IT department.

Hemingway Editor hemingwayapp.com Not AI in the chatbot sense, but a useful writing tool that highlights complex sentences, passive voice, and readability issues. Free to use in the browser. Good for making your academic writing clearer and more direct.

Zotero zotero.org A free, open-source reference manager. Not AI-powered, but essential for managing citations. Integrates with Word, Google Docs, and LibreOffice. If you're doing any amount of research, install Zotero. Your future self will thank you.

Study and Learning Tools

NotebookLM notebooklm.google.com Google's AI-powered notebook tool. Upload your course materials (PDFs, notes, slides) and NotebookLM will answer questions grounded in your specific documents. Free to use. Exceptionally useful for exam review because it stays focused on your actual course content, not the internet at large.

Anki apps.ankiweb.net A free, open-source spaced repetition flashcard app. Not AI-powered, but the gold standard for memorization. You can use AI to generate flashcard content (see Appendix A) and then import it into Anki for scientifically optimized review scheduling.

Quizlet (Free Tier) quizlet.com Flashcard and study tool with AI-powered features. The free tier includes basic flashcard creation and sharing. Quizlet's AI can generate practice questions from your study materials.

Wolfram Alpha wolframalpha.com A computational knowledge engine. Solves math problems, plots graphs, computes statistics, and answers factual questions with sourced data. Free to use for basic queries. The Pro version shows step-by-step solutions, which is valuable for math courses. Check if your school has a site license.

Coding and STEM Tools

GitHub Copilot (Free for Students) github.com/features/copilot AI-powered code completion and generation. Free for verified students through the GitHub Student Developer Pack. If you're taking any programming courses, this is worth setting up.

GitHub Student Developer Pack education.github.com/pack A collection of free developer tools for students, including GitHub Copilot, cloud credits, and more. Verify your student status to access. Not strictly an AI tool, but it includes AI tools and is free.

Google Colab colab.research.google.com Free cloud-based Jupyter notebooks with GPU access. If you're doing any data science, machine learning, or computational work, Colab lets you run code without installing anything. Free tier is generous for coursework.

Checking for Student Discounts and Free Access

Before you pay for any AI tool:

1. **Check your school's software portal.** Many universities negotiate site licenses for tools like Grammarly Premium, Microsoft Copilot, and others. Your IT department's software page is the first place to look.
2. **Check for student verification programs.** GitHub, JetBrains, Notion, and others offer free or discounted access for verified students. You'll need a .edu email address.
3. **Check the tool's pricing page.** Many AI tools have student pricing that isn't prominently advertised. Look for "Education," "Academic," or "Student" links at the bottom of pricing pages.
4. **Ask your department.** Some departments have budgets for student software access that they don't widely advertise.

Study Resources

Academic Writing

- *They Say / I Say* by Gerald Graff and Cathy Birkenstein — the best book on academic argumentation, period.
- The Purdue Online Writing Lab (OWL) — owl.purdue.edu — free, comprehensive guides to APA, MLA, Chicago, and academic writing in general.
- Your university's writing center — underused and undervalued. Go there.

Research Methods

- *The Craft of Research* by Wayne C. Booth, Gregory G. Colomb, and Joseph M. Williams — practical and readable.
- Your university's library website — librarians are research experts, and most offer one-on-one research consultations for free.

Critical Thinking About AI

- "On the Dangers of Stochastic Parrots" by Emily Bender et al. — a foundational paper on the limitations and risks of large language models.
- The AI Incident Database (incidentdatabase.ai) — a collection of real-world AI failures, useful for understanding what can go wrong.
- MIT Technology Review's AI section (technologyreview.com/ai) — consistently strong coverage of AI developments, accessible to non-experts.

Staying Current

- The AI landscape changes fast. Rather than list specific news sources that may shift in quality, here's the habit that matters: follow the official blogs of the AI companies whose tools you use (OpenAI, Anthropic, Google DeepMind). They announce new capabilities, limitations, and policy changes there first.

The AI for Everyone Series

This book is part of the AI for Everyone series by Finnoybu Press, built to help real people use AI tools effectively. Each title stands on its own, but they complement each other — if you find value in this book's approach, the others follow the same philosophy.

Collection 1: Core Tools

- ***ChatGPT: The Definitive Guide (2026 Edition)*** The comprehensive guide to ChatGPT for power users and professionals.

- ***ChatGPT: The Power User Guide (2026 Edition)*** Advanced workflows, custom GPTs, and API integration.

- ***Claude: The Definitive Guide (2026 Edition)*** Everything you need to know about Anthropic's Claude.

- ***Claude Code: The Power User Guide (2026 Edition)*** Deep dive into agentic development with Claude Code.

Collection 2: Essential Platforms

- ***Gemini: The Complete Guide (2026 Edition)*** Google's Gemini models, ecosystem, and integrations.
- ***Gemini: The Advanced Guide (2026 Edition)*** Advanced Gemini workflows, multimodal techniques, and Google Cloud integration.
- ***Microsoft Copilot: The Workplace AI Guide (2026 Edition)*** AI across the Microsoft 365 suite for everyday productivity.
- ***Microsoft Copilot: The Advanced Workplace Guide (2026 Edition)*** Advanced Copilot workflows, automation, and enterprise integration.
- ***Perplexity AI: The Research Playbook (2026 Edition)*** AI-powered research with real-time citations and source evaluation.
- ***Perplexity AI: The Advanced Research Playbook (2026 Edition)*** Advanced research workflows, deep analysis, and professional research techniques.

Collection 3: Authoritative Series

- ***AI Systems Playbook (2026 Edition)*** Architecture, integration, and operations for AI-powered systems.
- ***AI Prompt Engineering (2026 Edition)*** The complete guide to prompt engineering across models and use cases.
- ***AI for Developers (2026 Edition)*** Building better software with AI assistants.
- ***AI for Business (2026 Edition)*** The executive's guide to AI strategy, adoption, and governance.
- ***AI for Students (2026 Edition)*** — *this book*

All titles are available at **press.finnoybu.org** and through major book retailers. Visit **press.finnoybu.org** for the latest titles and updates.

A Note on Links and Longevity

AI tools change fast. URLs shift, products rebrand, free tiers adjust, new tools emerge. Every link and resource in this appendix was verified as of early 2026, but some will inevitably change. If a link is broken, search for the tool by name — it's almost certainly still available, just at a different address.

For the most current version of this resource list, visit **press.finnoybu.org/ai-for-students/resources**.

www.ingramcontent.com/pod-product-compliance
Ingram Content Group UK Ltd.
Pitfield, Milton Keynes, MK11 3LW, UK
UKHW051117290926
15471UKWH00010B/1717

9 798950 533181